Famous South African Crimes

Famous South African Crimes

Rob Marsh

Struik Timmins

Published by Struik Timmins Publishers
(a member of the Struik Group (Pty) Ltd)
Struik House
80 McKenzie Street
Cape Town
8001

Reg. No. 54/00965/07

First published in February 1991
Second impression August 1991
Third impression November 1992

Editors	Hilda Hermann and Angela Whittingham
Cover designer	Robert Meas
Cover photographer	Malcolm Dare
Designer	Jo Worthington-Smith DTP Design cc
DTP	Jo Worthington-Smith DTP Design cc
Reproduction	BellSet cc, Cape Town
Printing and binding	Unique Press (Pty) Ltd, Cape Town

ISBN 0 86978 448 X

CONTENTS

DEDICATION

With love to Pam, Robin, Helen and Sally

ACKNOWLEDGEMENTS

A number of people assisted me in the completion of this work. Special thanks are due to the library staff of *The Argus* newspaper, Cape Town, who kindly gave me access to their files and provided unstinting help during my research. A similar debt of gratitude is due to the staff of the South African Library, Queen Victoria Street, Cape Town. I would also like to express my thanks to the South African Police Force: I approached different detective units on a number of occasions and was always most courteously received and ably assisted.

INTRODUCTION

Most South Africans have heard of Marlene Lehnberg, the 'scissors murderess', and Andre Stander of the Stander Gang, and even Barend Strydom, the *Wit Wolf*. Some may even recall the theft of the Oppenheimer jewels in 1955 or the 'Bubbles' Schroeder mystery in 1949. But what of the Foster Gang? or Daisy de Melker? or Dorothea Kraft, the first woman hanged in the Union of South Africa? – yet these names are also part of South African criminal history.

All of the twenty-six cases documented in *Famous South African Crimes* are fascinating. Some are even world famous. The murder of Baron Dieter von Schauroth in 1961, for example, created a new class of murder: murder on request. Or there was the case of Ronnie Cohen in 1970, a Cape Town businessman, who was found guilty of murdering his wife and whose 'islands of memory' defence was extremely controversial. Or Duncan Donald Moodie, who is the only man in South African legal history who was tried, convicted and sentenced to death twice for the same crime.

Each chapter in *Famous South African Crimes* has been meticulously researched and carefully documented. It is perhaps not surprising, therefore, that the completion of this book has been a long and painstaking exercise. It has also been totally absorbing. If the reader gains even half the enjoyment from reading *Famous South African Crimes* as I did in writing it, then my endeavours have been worthwhile.

ROB MARSH

1.

MURDERING FOR MONEY

(PIERRE BASSON: 1903)

Pierre Corneille Faculys Basson was posthumously convicted of murder in 1906. He was described by Inspector Easton, the police officer who went to investigate his death, as 'a scoundrel from infancy'. Basson, who is believed to have killed eight or nine people was, in all probability, South Africa's first mass murderer.

Physically, Basson was unprepossessing – he had dark hair, deep-set brown eyes and was of average height and build – but he had a sharp mind and a keen nose for a shady deal. He was also violent and highly disturbed. He attacked a boy with a knife when he was only twelve, and he took pleasure in causing pain to animals. He liked to catch birds and torture them to death. He also chopped the feet off cats so that he could watch them writhe in agony.

In his teens, in Cape Town, Basson earned himself a reputation as a petty thief which led to bitter conflicts at home. When Basson's father died suddenly after a short illness, Pierre, who was then 17 or 18, showed little or no concern. However, the death of Mr Basson seems to have been a turning point for Pierre.

As head of the household – comprising his mother, two younger brothers and a younger sister – he now had the freedom (and a little insurance money) to enter a new and more lucrative field of criminal operations: insurance fraud.

Pierre's easy-money scheme involved money-lending. For this service, he charged the normal rate of interest and insisted that the lender take out a life insurance policy to cover the 'unexpected', naming himself as beneficiary. There was nothing unusual in this: it was normal business practice. The only difference between Pierre's operation and that of other money-lenders was that Pierre intended to make certain he collected the insurance money.

At first, Pierre kept things in the family. In 1901, he took out small life insurance policies for himself, his mother and his brother, Johan. Jasper, his youngest brother, was insured for £3 500, a huge amount at the time. This discrepancy, he argued, was to Jasper's advantage: in later years he would be able to borrow against the accumulated sum in the policy.

Within months, Basson had allowed all but Jasper's policy to lapse.

In February 1903, Pierre and Jasper decided to go fishing together at Gordon's Bay. Pierre went down a day before his brother and booked in at the Holloway Hotel.

Mr Holloway, the owner of the hotel, would later recall when being questioned by insurance assessors that Pierre had been particularly interested in drowning incidents in the area. Mr Holloway remembered telling him about someone named Roux who had lost his life at a spot called Ruigte Vlei not long before. He also mentioned a particularly notorious spot called Sewing-room Rock where there was a vicious undercurrent and victims vanished without trace. Pierre, he recalled, asked if the men had been washed off the rock and why none of the victims had ever been found. These apparently innocuous questions were later to assume great significance.

Jasper Basson arrived at Gordon's Bay late on the afternoon of Friday, 13 February, 1903. The two brothers left the hotel to go fishing before light the next morning. At about 6.45 a.m., two other early-morning fishermen, Mr August Deydier and Dr Ford, met Pierre, who was walking back towards the hotel. He had two rods over his shoulder.

'There has been a great accident,' Basson said. 'My brother Jasper's been drowned. He was cutting bait when a tremendous wave swept him off the rocks. I heard him give a cry for help, but another wave washed over me and threw me into a gully. I spotted him once, face downwards in the water, then he vanished from view. He did not come up again.'

Mr Deydier and Dr Ford looked at each other. Pierre's calmness struck Mr Deydier most strongly. He would have expected someone who had just witnessed a family disaster to show signs of distress or confusion, but Pierre was in total control of himself. And Basson's account of the incident made him even more suspicious. If the second wave, that had prevented him from going to his brother's assistance, had driven him into a gully between the rocks, how was it that only one of Basson's trouser-legs was wet?

A search party was organized. Basson and a number of local fishermen took to a rowing boat and set out along the coast. When they reached Sewing-room Rock, Basson pointed to the spot where his brother had disappeared. There was no sign of the body.

Despite an extensive search, Jasper Basson was never seen again.

Shortly after returning to Cape Town, Basson notified the insurance company of his brother's death. By this time, a number of unpleasant rumours were circulating. To make matters worse, the insurance company instituted an inquiry and discovered that Basson had attempted to get Mr G. Kruse, the barman at the Holloway Hotel, to make a false statement concerning the sequence of events on the fateful morning. Kruse had initially agreed to sign an affidavit. However, when Basson subsequently arrived with a Justice of the Peace, Kruse found that the account of the incident which Basson had prepared bore so little resemblance to the truth that, despite an inducement of £25, he declined to sign.

The insurance company refused to pay out – because of the unsatisfactory evidence of Jasper's death 'by violent, accidental, external and visible means'. In other words, it was indirectly accusing the family of fraud (not murder). At Pierre's insistence, Mrs Basson took the insurance company to court. Ultimately, the case went to the Supreme Court and judgment was pronounced in Basson's favour. With the payout, the Bassons bought a house called *The Arums* in Heatherton Road, Claremont.

It would seem that Basson's success with the insurance company encouraged him to repeat his scheme a number of times. One man who had ceded his life insurance policy, worth £375, to Basson was found dead on Woodstock beach. There was some indication that he had been throttled to death. Another of Basson's clients drowned while the two of them were out sailing together. A German couple by the name of Smit, who were acquaintances of Basson, were also shot and robbed, and there was evidence that linked them to Basson. He is also believed to have been responsible for the death of a man named Adolf Beck, whose body was found floating in the Black River.

Between 1902 and 1905, Basson conceived a number of ingenious schemes designed to trick people out of their money. Then, towards the end of 1905, he met a German farmer named Wilhelm Schaefer. This meeting would have disastrous consequences for both men, and would lead to what became known as *The Schaefer Affair*.

Wilhelm Schaefer owned a farm, *Highlands*, about twenty-five kilometres from Claremont, at the end of the Klipfontein Road. Schaefer, who was 54, was a frugal and industrious man. He shared the property with his brother, Gottlieb.

When Basson learnt that Schaefer was looking to sell *Highlands*, he made up his mind to swindle him out of the property. In December 1905, Basson went to see Schaefer and made an offer to purchase the farm. Schaefer insisted that the asking price was £1 400, but, after some hard bargaining, the two men agreed on a price of £1 020. Schaefer explained that once full payment for the property had been made, legal transfer of ownership would take place. To this end, the two men visited Schaefer's Cape Town attorney, Hermann Hirschberg.

Schaefer made one important provision at this stage in the transaction: transfer was not to take place unless he was present. In other words, he did not want the deed of transfer passed to Basson without proof of payment.

A few days after the initial meeting, Basson called at Hirschberg's office and tried to get him to transfer the property into his name. The attorney refused.

Basson was disappointed, but not discouraged: he was convinced he could outwit the attorney.

A week later, Basson visited Hirschberg's office a third time. On this occasion, he announced that he had paid Schaefer for the farm and again asked the attorney to transfer the property into his name. Hirschberg refused, since Basson had neither receipt nor any other proof of payment.

He did agree to prepare all the necessary documents for signature, however, and provided Basson with draft documents of the intended sale, which he could present to the Board of Executors to substantiate his application for a loan of £500. (Shortly after this, the Board approved the loan, subject to a bond being passed for *Highlands*.)

Early in January 1906, Basson arrived at Hirschberg's office with a receipt for the outstanding £1 020. Although Hirschberg was unaware that the receipt was counterfeit, he did explain that, as a formality, he would have to contact Schaefer before final transfer could be made. Naturally, Basson objected to this. The seller was quite satisfied, he claimed; besides, he had gone to Kimberley, so it was impossible to contact him.

Despite the fact that he held power of attorney, Hirschberg stood his ground and refused to transfer ownership. Then Basson withdrew a cheque for £850 from his pocket, claiming that the money had been given to him by his mother towards payment for the property. By this time, Hirschberg's suspicions were fully aroused. He declared himself unhappy with the whole affair, and refused to proceed with the transaction until he had spoken to Schaefer personally. Basson stormed out of his office.

It was evident to Basson that his carefully planned scheme to defraud Schaefer was going badly wrong. He reasoned that his only recourse was to murder Schaefer, hide his body, and forge his signature on the relevant documents. To this end, he immediately began making preparations in earnest. As soon as he reached home, he sent his gardener, Martin Cherrick, to fetch a labourer, named Peter Christian, from a nearby brickyard. Basson set Christian to digging a large pit in the chicken run in the back yard. To his mother, Basson gave the explanation that the pit was being dug for pipes which were to be laid to improve the drainage system. He said that since he hadn't obtained permission for the scheme from the local council, it had to be conducted in secret.

A week later, the pit was complete. He then obtained two bags of lime, which he stored inside the hencoop. The next step in Basson's plan was to acquire chloroform with which to drug his victim. He used a false name to obtain this from a pharmacist in Long Street. (It would later emerge that Basson had obtained cyanide from the same source on two previous occasions.)

The stage was set, and Basson summoned his victim to Claremont. On 22 January, 1906, Wilhelm Schaefer set out by horse-and-trap for Basson's home. *En route*, he stopped at Herbert Hawkins' blacksmith shop in Lansdowne Road and asked Hawkins to shoe his horses and make some minor repairs to his carriage.

'I'll be back in one or two hours,' he said, 'after I've collected the money for my farm from Pierre Basson.' Then he set off on foot.

When Schaefer arrived at *The Arums,* he was met by Basson and a friend of his named Tobias Louw. The three men went into Basson's room together. Schaefer was never seen alive again.

What happened to him? A possible scenario is that he was first plied with drink, then overpowered and murdered by Basson, possibly with the help of Louw. After that, his body must have been kept hidden inside the house until nightfall. Then, when everyone else had gone to bed, the two men would have stripped their victim before carrying his body out through the back door in Pierre's room, which opened onto the yard, and across to the large hencoop. (Ironically, Mrs Basson would later explain that she had assumed that Schaefer had left the house this way.) It just so happened that a local charwoman, Catherine Caroline Josephine Mochella, was passing by the yard just as the two men set to work. She heard suspicious noises, spotted the feeble light the two men were using, and, thinking that someone was in the act of stealing Basson's birds, cautiously crept forward to investigate. Through a gap in the wall she saw what looked like the white body of a man being tumbled into a large hole in the ground. 'Give me the lime,' she heard Basson hiss.

Alarmed by what she had seen, Mochella crept away and went home. She didn't contact the police because she was afraid they would put her in prison 'for nothing'.

In another part of Claremont, Hawkins the blacksmith was also perturbed because Schaefer had not returned to collect his property. The next morning, he rode into Claremont and called at the police station, then went to Basson's house.

Mrs Basson told him that she thought Schaefer had left for Kimberley the previous afternoon. This didn't sound right to Hawkins, but he nevertheless returned to his shop.

Shortly thereafter, Basson himself arrived to take possession of Schaefer's horse-and-trap. He produced a receipt for £1 020, purportedly signed by Schaefer, claiming that he owned all of the German's property, and then paid for the repairs. What most surprised Hawkins was that the receipt was dated 11 January. Yet, the previous day (22 January) Schaefer had said he was in town to receive payment for the farm. It didn't seem to make sense to Hawkins that a cautious man like Schaefer would issue a receipt without first receiving payment.

Within days of Schaefer's disappearance, Basson moved to *Highlands* and began going through Schaefer's papers. Gottlieb, the dead man's brother, protested vehemently, but Basson merely brandished the receipt and reiterated his claim that he had bought the farm 'lock, stock and barrel'. In a magnanimous gesture, he agreed to let Gottlieb remain on the farm until he got on his feet.

To those who knew him, Schaefer's disappearance was a complete mystery. The police were approached to investigate the matter, but without a body or any hard evidence, there was little they could do. The newspapers, however, were free to speculate. In *The Argus* of 7 February, there was a story which read:

CAPE FLATS MYSTERY
MURDER THEORY FAVOURED
INFORMATION VOLUNTEERED

The whereabouts of Schaefer, the Cape Flats farmer, is still a mystery. Every nerve has been strained by the police to elucidate the circumstances that passed from the time that Schaefer left the premises of Hawkins the blacksmith at Claremont and there is more than a possibility that Schaefer's disappearance will be followed by some startling revelations.

Two days later, on 9 February, the police offered a £50 reward to anyone who could offer information which would help resolve the mystery of Schaefer's disappearance. The missing man was described as: 'German, aged 54, unmarried, height 5 feet 7 inches. Medium build, broad shouldered, stoops when walking. Light brown cast in one eye. Was wearing, when last seen, a dirty grey jacket suit, striped cotton shirt with collar, brown tie with white spots, an old brown felt hat and old yellow Blucher boots.'

For three weeks there was no response. Then Caroline Mochella sent an anonymous note to the head of the CID. It read:

Go and search Mr P. Bassons fowlrun for the missing man. Dig the grown up Heatherton Avenue for Mr Schafer the missing man.

She waited for a response in the newspapers, but nothing happened. In desperation, she wrote a second letter:

Sir this is the hole story of the missing man Mr Shafer the first notice I send was for the police to no that the missing man is on the property of

Mr P Basson in his fowlhock under the floor there is a lot of sand on the top Not the hock but where they sleep in.

On 10 February, an interview with Basson appeared in *The Argus*, in which he denied any knowledge of Schaefer's disappearance. He had agreed to the interview, he claimed, because of the stories that were circulating and the 'garbled and unfair stuff published in some papers'.

On the same day, the police received Caroline Mochella's second note. In response, Inspector Easton, Detective Head Constable Walker, Detective-Sergeant Bree and two other detectives immediately went to *The Arums*, where they began to dig up the hencoop.

Pierre, who had hidden in his bedroom, emerged after about ten minutes. He was accosted by his brother, Johan.

'They're digging up the fowlhouse, Pierre!' Johan said. There was a wild look of despair on Pierre's face.

'It was Louw,' he whispered. 'The police will find the body if they dig deep enough. I'll be arrested; they'll arrest me. The detectives will find Schaefer's body and they will bring Louw and me into it. We did it together....' He then returned to his room.

Shortly afterwards, his mother went in to him. He kissed her.

'I'm going to get dressed for the police,' he said. 'I have done no wrong. It was Toby's show.'

However, only moments after she had left, a shot rang out. He had put a gun to his head and committed suicide.

In the Sporting Edition of *The Argus* that same night, under the heading *'Flats Mystery Solved'*, an article described events after the police had begun to dig up the hencoop at Basson's house at about 2.45 p.m. 'A strong smell gave [the] indication that developments were at hand,' the article explained. Eventually Schaefer's body was found. It was 'immersed in quick-lime, in an advanced stage of decomposition but was easily recognisable'.

So, Pierre Basson was never brought to trial for his crimes. His accomplice, Louw, was subsequently tried for murder, but there was insufficient evidence against him and he was acquitted. On 1 March, Mrs Basson was also arrested, remanded in Roeland Street Jail for a week, and then released.

The closing chapter of this grisly saga was played out some months later. After Pierre's death, the family was destitute and *The Arums* and its contents were sold by public auction. It is rather interesting that the event attracted over 1 500 people and the goods on sale fetched outrageous prices, far in excess of their real value. Perhaps crime does pay after all...

2.

PUBLIC ENEMY NUMBER ONE

(THE FOSTER GANG: 1914)

William Robert Clem Foster was born in 1886 and grew up in East Griqualand. He came from a respectable middle-class family. His father was Irish and his mother was a South African who came from Grahamstown. He went to a good school, showed above-average intelligence, was popular with his schoolmates and good at sport. After leaving school, he studied mine surveying for a time, and then decided to make his living as a photographer. As an adult, Foster proved himself to be a loving husband, a faithful friend and a devoted father.

So, how was it that, as leader of the Foster Gang, he became involved in the murder of five people – including three policemen – caused the death of five more, crippled one innocent bystander and, for three months from July to September 1914, had the dubious distinction of being *Public Enemy Number One*?

Despite his apparently balanced background, Foster was a complicated man who was volatile and headstrong and, later on, bitterly resentful of authority. Even so, his descent into violent crime seems to have occurred slowly and by degrees.

Foster's first brush with the law occurred in Durban in March 1908, where, at the age of twenty-two, he got drunk and ended up in a brawl. When the police eventually arrived to quell the disturbance, Foster chose to resist arrest rather than go quietly. He was overpowered, locked up for the night in the local jail, and fined £3 at the magistrates' court the following day.

Some months later, he was caught travelling by train without a ticket. Again he resisted arrest, and then compounded the offence by attempting to run away. He was apprehended and charged. This time, the magistrate took a dim view of his behaviour. He was fined £10 and sent to prison for a month for 'escaping from justice'.

After serving his sentence, William Foster went to South West Africa (*now Namibia*), but before the year was out he was in trouble again. This time he was prosecuted for stealing donkeys. In his defence he said that he had planned to sell them in order to obtain enough money to return to British soil. On 12 October, 1908, he was sentenced at De Aar to six months in prison.

In 1909, Foster returned to Johannesburg, where he seemed to settle down for a time. He took up surveying and photography once more, and became a keen cyclist. However, given his now entrenched resentment of authority and his bitter grudge against the police, it probably was inevitable that he would run into more trouble before long.

In 1912, Foster made a trip to England. When he returned to South Africa early in 1913, he struck up a friendship with a colourful character named John Maxim, alias Maxwell, a man who was to have a great influence on his life. Maxim was an ex-rodeo star and sharp-shooter. He had come to South Africa from America with a travelling show and had decided to stay on. The two men determined to move up in the world together.

Foster and Maxim travelled to Cape Town, took lodgings in the city, and planned the armed robbery of The American Swiss Watch Company, which was situated in Longmarket Street. They were soon joined by Foster's brother, Jimmy, and a fourth man named Jack Johnson.

At first, the gang stayed at Claridges Hotel (since demolished) in the suburb of Gardens, but later moved to a boarding establishment, Ebenezer House, in Hope Street, where they believed they would be less conspicuous.

By Wednesday, 19 March, 1913, everything had been prepared. At 6.45 p.m., they set out for the American Swiss Watch Company wearing false beards and moustaches. The two owners of the jewellery shop, Mr I. Hirschsohn and Mr Abraham Grusd, were still at work in the shop. They had pulled down the window blinds but had not locked the heavy security gates.

Hirschsohn and Grusd looked up in surprise when Foster and his three accomplices walked into the room where they were working. Foster waved a powerful handgun at them. 'Don't move or we'll shoot,' he warned.

Hirschsohn was bound, gagged and hooded, while Grusd was forced at gunpoint to open all the safes. Within minutes, the robbers had taken almost £5 000 worth of watches, rings and jewellery.

'We have a watchman outside,' Foster said as the four men were leaving. 'He'll shoot anyone who comes out of this shop in the next fifteen minutes.' Hirscholm eventually managed to free himself. He removed the hood from his partner's head, then hobbled outside, still in the ankle chains the robbers had used to fetter him, and raised the alarm. Within minutes, the police arrived.

Detectives from the CID conducted an intensive investigation of the area, but the thieves had left few clues behind them.

Immediately after the robbery, Foster packed the stolen goods in one holdall, his burglar's outfit in another, and put both bags in a large leather cabin trunk.

Then he called a taxi to take him to the left-luggage office at the station.

In 1913, the cost of leaving an item in left-luggage was twopence. Foster wanted to leave the trunk, a typewriter case, a portmanteau and an overcoat, at a total cost of 8d. However, it wasn't until he got to the station that he realised that he had only a gold sovereign (worth the equivalent of R250) on him. Ernest Sephton, the left-luggage attendant, couldn't change such a large amount, and suggested that Foster obtain change at the booking-office. Foster became unreasonable, refusing to leave his articles at the office without a receipt of some sort. Eventually, Sephton agreed to give him the four tickets without payment.

'You go and get change and then come back and pay me,' he said. Foster agreed. Minutes later, he returned with the money he owed and complimented Sephton on showing such trust.

This incident was Foster's first serious mistake – he had committed the professional criminal's cardinal sin: that of drawing attention to himself.

Lodging at Ebenezer House at the same time as Foster and his companions was a man named Harry Bloom. In his time, Harry had been an actor and singer, and he knew Cape Town's relatively small entertainment community well. So, when the four strangers claimed to be music-hall artists appearing at the Tivoli or Opera House, he knew they were lying. When the group suddenly departed on the morning after the robbery, Harry's worst suspicions were confirmed, and he contacted the police.

On searching Foster's room, the police found a number of clues which linked the men to the robbery at the American Swiss Watch Company.

They interviewed John Gallias, the taxi-driver who had taken Foster to the station, and before long they were talking to Ernest Sephton. When the police eventually opened Foster's luggage, they had all the evidence they needed.

Meanwhile, the owners of the American Swiss Watch Company offered the substantial reward of £500 for information leading to the arrest of the robbers. The offer of reward appeared in the *Cape Times* on the morning of Friday, 21 March.

Three days after the robbery, on the morning of Saturday, 22 March, Foster strolled up to the left-luggage counter, handed over his tickets and was immediately arrested. He was carrying in his pocket a set of keys which belonged to the American Swiss Watch Company and a loaded Mauser pistol. He also had two firearm licences in his possession, one in the name of Robert Ward Jackson and the other in his own name. After being interviewed by detectives from the CID, he was locked up in Roeland Street Jail. The hunt for his accomplices continued.

Not long after, Foster's brother, Jimmy, and one of their accomplices, Jack Johnson, were arrested in Johannesburg. Maxim escaped arrest.

While in Roeland Street Jail awaiting trial, Foster married a dark-eyed beauty named Peggy, whom he had known for about two years. The service was conducted in the prison chapel under special licence. A local minister performed the ceremony, and the chief warder and another prison official acted as witnesses.

The first hearing concerning the robbery took place on 23 March, 1913. On this occasion, Foster was alone in the dock, but at the next hearing, held on 13 April, he was joined by his brother and Johnson. All three men were committed for trial.

The trial began on 22 May, 1913, presided over by Sir John Kotze.

Robert Foster expected Jimmy to get away with a light sentence, but he was unaware that the robbery was not his younger brother's first offence – in fact, Jimmy had served a three-month prison sentence just the previous year.

Each of the three men was sentenced to 12 years hard labour. Peggy Foster, who had been at the trial every day, was barely able to gasp, 'I'll wait for you, Chummy,' before she collapsed and had to be helped from the court.

Foster's reaction to the sentence was one of fury. He considered it a travesty of justice: despite the fact that he had organized and led the robbery, Jimmy was being equally punished. From that day on, it seems, he was determined to get back at the system that had imposed such harsh and unfair punishment.

It is also interesting to note that this trial led to a precedent being set under South African law, in terms of the granting of reward money (*see box*).

Robert Foster, Jimmy Foster and Jack Johnson were duly incarcerated in Pretoria Prison. Nine months later, in February 1914, Foster escaped while working in a prison gang. Shortly after this, he teamed up with John Maxim and Carl Mezar, alias George Smit, a twenty-two-year-old with a long criminal record. For the three months from July to September 1914, the Foster Gang, as the trio became known, went on an orgy of robbery and violence the likes of which South Africans had never seen before.

On 17 July, the Foster Gang began their campaign of terror by attempting to rob the Boksburg North branch of the National Bank.

They were breaking into the bank when they were surprised by a clerk who slept on the premises. Carl Mezar immediately attacked the man and a fierce struggle ensued. The clerk managed to get away, and rushed towards the Boksburg North Hotel on the street corner opposite, shouting for help. The commotion drew a barman named Alex Charlson to the scene. When Charlson tried to intervene, he was shot in the chest. He died an hour later.

Their plan was to get into the bank by breaking through the wall of the building next door, but, just as they were about to enter the bank, the man who had hired the room they were using returned.

Out on the street, an onlooker who attempted to prevent the robbers from escaping was shot in the leg and crippled for life. The Foster Gang escaped on a motorcycle.

A few weeks later, the gang successfully robbed Roodepoort Post Office. This was followed by a second post office robbery, this time at Vredendorp. Then, in the early hours of Sunday, 13 September, at the Big Bottle Store on the corner of Viljoen and Kimberley Roads in Doornfontein, there began a sequence of events which ultimately was to lead to nine deaths and the most intensive manhunt the South African Police had ever conducted.

When the robbers attempted to break into the Big Bottle Store, they triggered an electric alarm which alerted a night watchman who was sleeping inside the building. The man tried to scare the burglars away by rapping on a windowpane with a key. Then he saw a beat policeman approaching and tapped more vigorously to attract his attention. The constable heard him, approached to investigate, and was attacked by the three robbers and knocked unconscious. Foster and the others then ran off, and the night watchman rushed to the local police station.

At 4.15 the next morning, in another part of the town, Ser-

Who gets the reward?

Following the successful prosecution of the three robbers, Harry Bloom, John Gallias and Ernest Sephton came forward and claimed the £500 reward which the American Swiss Watch Company had offered. Harry Bloom, who had summoned the police to Ebenezer House straight after the robbery, had the strongest claim. However, it transpired that he had contacted the police before the reward had been offered. (Bloom contacted the police on the morning after the robbery, that is Thursday, 20 March.

The offer of reward only appeared in the Cape Times on the following morning, Friday, 21 March.) In 1915, the Supreme Court advised the company that they were under no obligation to pay the reward to anyone, thereby establishing the principle that no-one can claim a reward from another unless a definite contract exists between them.

The publication in a newspaper or the announcement on TV of a reward offer, which is common practice these days, constitutes such a contract. However, it remains true that anyone who aids the authorities in bringing a criminal to justice is not eligible for a reward if the information is provided prior to an offer of reward being made.

At the request of the authorities we reproduce photographs of the three men wanted by the Police for the dastardly murders of two policemen on Saturday night at Fairview. The names of the men in the order in which they appear are Robert Ward Jackson, alias Foster, John Maxim, alias Maxwell, and Carl Mezar, alias George Smit.

Reproduced with permission *The Star*

The Foster Gang

geant Neil McCloud, who was on patrol with Constable Swanepoel, spotted a man (Maxim) sitting on a bench opposite the Imperial Bottle Store. On being questioned, he claimed to be waiting for a tram to go to work. The policemen searched him anyway and, finding a loaded revolver and housebreaking tools in his pockets, duly arrested the man. However, just as the three men were passing the Imperial Bottle Store, Maxim suddenly began shouting for help. A moment later, Foster emerged from the side of the building, brandishing a revolver. 'Hands up! Release that man!' he demanded.

Instead of doing as he was told, Sergeant McCloud ordered Constable Swanepoel to draw the gun they had taken from Maxim. Shots rang out. Foster was hurt, but McCloud fell to the ground mortally injured. As Swanepoel ran off to seek assistance, the three robbers escaped by motorcycle.

Minutes later, police reinforcements were on the scene. Then, in nearby Eleanor Street, the body of Sergeant Robert Mansfield was discovered. Like McCloud, Mansfield had been shot dead.

The evidence indicated that he had been investigating a noise inside the building where the three robbers were at work when he was shot, probably by Mezar: a trail of blood extended from a spot near a blown safe to where Mansfield's body was found in the street.

A massive manhunt was set in motion for the three men whom *The Star* newspaper dubbed 'The Motorcycle Bandits'. It was not long before a woman living in Regent's Park contacted the police to say that she knew where the men were staying. They had taken a small cottage on the corner of Bob Street and South Road, she said. She had first become suspicious when she noticed that the men avoided neighbours and seemed to come and go at odd hours of the day and night. Then she had recognized them as the wanted men from their pictures in the newspaper.

Three plain-clothes officers were sent to investigate. Detective Mynott, who was in charge of the contingent, warily approached the back yard. Sure enough, over the fence he spotted the criminals working on a motor car. Instead of waiting for assistance to arrive, Mynott decided to arrest the Foster Gang himself.

Having dispatched Detective Layde to the front of the house and Constable Murphy to the rear, Mynott went and knocked on the front door. Receiving no reply, he opened the door, walked through the house and out into the yard at the back.

> *On the East Rand, a Dr Gerald Grace, who was rushing to answer an urgent call, failed to stop at a roadblock and the police, thinking that he was a member of the Foster Gang, fired into the car, killing him outright and wounding his wife.*
>
> *On the other side of the Reef, General Jacobus Hercules de la Rey, who, it would later emerge, was on his way to Potchefstoom to start a rebellion amongst the troops there, was shot dead when he ordered his chauffeur to drive through a roadblock. He was also mistaken for a member of the Foster Gang.*

'Put your hands up!' he ordered. Instead of being thrown into a state of panic, Foster, Maxim and Mezar remained cool and collected. Without turning around, Foster began to try to bluster his way out of the situation; in this brief interim, Maxim quietly handed him a gun.

Detective Layde shouted a warning to Mynott just as Foster turned and fired – but too late. As Mynott fell to the ground, fatally wounded, his pistol fired, the bullet hitting the car. Within a matter of seconds, Foster had grabbed his wife and child and started the car. As the vehicle roared down the driveway, Maxim and Mezar threw themselves aboard.

Within hours of Mynott's death, every policeman on the Reef was looking for the Foster Gang. Roadblocks were set up on every route in and out of the city, themselves causing a couple of bizarre deaths (*see box*).

Eventually, the car in which the gang had escaped from Regent's Park was found abandoned on the old road which ran behind the Primrose cemetery, near

Photograph courtesy of *Huisgenoot*

Mrs Peggy Foster

Bezuidenhout Valley, with a bullet in the gearbox. The police brought in tracker dogs and the search was intensified.

Meanwhile, Foster (who was wounded), Mezar and Maxim had taken refuge in a cave in the Kensington koppies that Foster had known as a boy. Foster's wife and child had gone to a safe house in Germiston.

On the afternoon of 16 September, 1914, a search party led by Sergeant Thomas Granger and Lance-Corporal Sergeant discovered the gang's hiding place. Without reinforcements, however, they couldn't flush the men out, so they rolled rocks in front of the cave mouth, effectively sealing it, then sent for their superiors and mounted a guard.

Within hours, the cave was surrounded by a heavy cordon of police and hundreds of sightseers. The police first attempted to drive the robbers into the open by lowering teargas cannisters on ropes to the entrance of the cave, but the wind blew the gas towards the onlookers, forcing the police to give up the venture. As night fell, floodlights were brought in.

The next morning, the police were in the process of removing some of the boulders from the cave entrance when a shot rang out: Mezar had committed suicide.

About an hour after this, Foster came to the cave entrance. 'I want to see Peggy,' he said.

'Where is she?' asked Detective Martin, the man in charge of the operation. Foster gave them the address in Germiston where his wife was in hiding. At about two o'clock in the afternoon, she was brought to the cave entrance.

'I only want to have a chat with her,' Foster said. 'After that we'll send our guns out and surrender.' For a while the police debated the wisdom of allowing Mrs Foster to join her husband. It was obvious that none of the robbers could escape and it seemed a small concession to make, particularly if it meant that the deadlock could be resolved without further bloodshed.

Half an hour after Peggy Foster had entered the cave, Foster spoke to the police once more. He wanted to say farewell to his mother and father and two sisters, who were also waiting nearby.

In the gloom of the cave entrance Foster, who, according to his father, was 'garnered up', introduced Maxim to his family. 'This is the man who has stuck to me right through,' he told them.

'Judge Kotze is to blame for all of this,' he said. 'And I didn't want to kill Mynott either. He fired at me first and I had to defend myself. What could we do?' he asked. 'It was them or us.'

He then announced that Maxim and he had decided to commit suicide in order to avoid being hanged.

'I'm going to stay with you, Chummy,' Peggy Foster said. Foster didn't argue. He bounced his five-month-old baby daughter on his knee for a few moments then, handing her over to his sister, said, 'The rest of you had better be going now.' A suicide pact had been formed.

A few minutes after Foster's family had left the cave, three shots rang out. Maxim had acted as executioner, shooting first his two companions and then himself.

In the cave, the police discovered a box of stamps linking the gang to post office robberies at Roodepoort and Bellevue.

The saga of the Foster Gang had finally ended – or so it seemed. Yet, there is one last twist to this unusual tale.

The police inspector who had permitted Peggy Foster to join her husband in the cave subsequently became so overwrought at what he perceived to have been a serious error of judgement on his part that he too committed suicide. He was the Foster Gang's eleventh victim.

AN INTRIGUING POSTSCRIPT

In June 1937, a man named Andries du Plessis was arrested at Strubenvale by Detective Michiel Ackermann and charged with murder. He was accompanied by a woman who would later claim to be the daughter of Robert and Peggy Foster.

At his trial, Du Plessis maintained that the woman was innocent of any involvement, and she was allowed to go free. When, after Du Plessis's conviction, the woman went to Detective Ackermann to collect some of her lover's belongings, she made a number of startling revelations.

She maintained that she had been married to a policeman and had lived in the Eastern Cape – until she had met a miner with whom she had moved to Durban. She had subsequently left this man to go to the Rand, where she had met and fallen for Du Plessis. She had been attracted by his impulsive, reckless nature, she said. After Du Plessis had left his wife for her, she claimed, they carried out a number of robberies together. At first, the woman said, she simply acted as lookout, but later she became more involved. Du Plessis had murdered seven people (not five as the police suspected); she had merely searched their pockets and belongings. However, she confessed that she had shot and killed the eighth victim herself.

Detective Ackermann could find no evidence to link the woman to the killings, and had to release her. She disappeared and was never heard of again. From the information the woman had supplied, he was certain of one thing, though, and that was that she was the daughter of Robert and Peggy Foster.

If she was, we can only theorize as to what caused her to follow in the footsteps of her notorious father, Robert Foster. But only she really knows – if she is still alive…

3.

WHEN WITCHCRAFT FAILS

(DOROTHEA KRAFT: 1918)

Dorothea van der Merwe (or Kraft as she was known at the time of her crime) was the first woman hanged in the Union of South Africa. She died for her part in the murder of Louis Tumpowski, which had taken place at her farm in the Transvaal in 1918.

Having read her story, you may well question whether she deserved this historic distinction. Was she really a scheming hard-nosed woman, who deserved the ultimate punishment? Or was she merely a casualty of her age? A victim of exploitation? Would a modern judge, given the laws of the time, be likely to pass the same sentence on her?

Dorothea Kraft first met Louis Tumpowski when he visited her farm looking to buy fresh produce for his thriving general dealer business.

Tumpowski, a Jewish emigrant from the United States, arrived in South Africa in 1887, at the age of twenty-five. On his arrival, he headed for Johannesburg, which at that time was a small but rapidly expanding mining town. Recognizing that the area offered great potential for the small entrepreneur, Tumpowski set himself up selling general provisions. Although he had several sources of supply, he would regularly tour farms and small-holdings in the locality in the quest for fresh supplies.

The widowed Mrs Kraft had a very different life. Although she owned her farm, *Treurfontein*, in the Lichtenberg district, it provided her and her daughter, Polly, with little more than a subsistence existence. It was a small and unattractive place, and drought and poor soil meant unrelenting hard work. To add to her problems, the local people she employed as labourers resented taking orders from a woman. Mrs Kraft confided in Tumpowski that she needed a man around the property, a manager who could run the place. She asked him to keep his ears and eyes open for such a person.

On a subsequent visit, Tumpowski offered to lease and run *Treurfontein* himself, at a rent of £25 per year. Mrs Kraft found this proposal agreeable and, at Tumpowski's suggestion, a contract was drawn up by a firm of Johannesburg attorneys to make the arrangement legal and binding. The document was signed on 21 May, 1914.

Tumpowski moved to *Treurfontein*, where he and Mrs Kraft soon began living together as man and wife. Despite these changes, the farm failed to prosper. In 1918, Mrs Kraft decided that the time had come to sell the property. It was only then that she learnt from Tumpowski that the agreement between them contained an option clause giving him the right, at lease end, to purchase the farm from her at a price of £3 5s a morgen. (A morgen is approximately two acres.) This in effect meant that she was compelled to sell to Tumpowski, and at a price well below market value.

Mrs Kraft was highly indignant, maintaining that this option clause had been omitted when the terms of the agreement were read out to her. Nevertheless, the firm of attorneys which she approached to look into her legal position simply confirmed what Tumpowski had already told her – that she was obliged to sell the farm to him and at the bargain price.

Finding herself in this legal trap, Mrs Kraft decided to appeal to Tumpowski's better nature. She believed that if she were to marry Tumpowski, she could have the option clause quashed in an antenuptial agreement. However, by this time relations between them had become so strained that Tumpowski refused even to consider the possibility of marriage. When this failed, she turned to her second option: witchcraft. She approached a local witch-doctor named Jim Bird (also known as *Whiskers*) and asked for a love potion which would cause Tumpowski to fall madly in love with her. Unfortunately, when she put some of this potion into Tumpowski's tea he became violently ill and accused her of trying to poison him. After this incident he refused to take food from her.

By this time, the deterioration in their relationship had become common knowledge in the district. One witness at her trial claimed that Dorothea had wanted to know where she could get hold of a substance which would give Tumpowski a 'loathsome disease', and another claimed that the accused had asked him how much it would cost to kill 'the old Jew'. Neither of the witnesses had taken the threats seriously, however.

When the love potion failed, Mrs Kraft went back to Jim Bird. This time, she wanted something to get rid of the man. Ideally, she wanted him merely driven away from the farm; failing all else, she wanted him dead. For magic of this strength, Bird explained, some small personal effects (including a lock of hair) belonging to Tumpowski were required. Mrs Kraft obliged, and Bird placed the items in a matchbox. After incanting a spell, Bird instructed Mrs Kraft to bury the matchbox beneath the threshold of Tumpowski's room. When he crossed the threshold, the spell would take effect and Tumpowski would weaken and die, Bird promised.

By the time it had become clear to her that Bird's magic had failed for a second time, Mrs Kraft was desperate. It is at this point that Hermanus Lambertus Swartz enters the saga.

Swartz, who was in love with Polly Kraft, was a regular visitor to the farm and he viewed Mrs Kraft's plight with a great deal of sympathy. He reasoned that the solution to the problem lay in a more direct approach. Mrs Kraft agreed and together they determined to have Tumpowski murdered.

Jim Bird was prepared to perform the deed in return for a payment of £100. On the night of 2 February, 1918, during a violent hailstorm, Mrs Kraft, Hermanus Swartz, Jim Bird and three local labourers assembled in the living-room of the farmhouse. Speaking in low tones, they made final preparations. Finally, Swartz took Bird to the door of Tumpowski's room, quietly worked the latch, then pushed the witch-doctor inside. Tumpowski barely had a chance to look up in surprise before Bird attacked him with a knobkerrie. Blow after blow rained down on the victim's skull. Yet, when Bird stepped back from the bed, Swartz was convinced the man was still alive. He tied a leather thong around Tumpowski's neck and cut his throat with a pocket knife. Mrs Kraft fetched a blanket, which she used to stem the flow of blood.

At this point, Jim Bird, convinced that someone was watching through the window, suddenly took fright. Disregarding the offer of a further £100 if he would use his magic to conceal the crime, he ran off into the night.

With the help of the three African labourers – Hermanus, Andries and Piccanin – Mrs Kraft and Swartz then carried Tumpowski's body outside and buried it in a rough grave beneath an ash-pit in the garden. By daylight, all evidence of the crime had been removed.

After the murder, Mrs Kraft began to complain that she had been deserted by Tumpowski, and for a short time even went to stay with a neighbour because, she said, she was afraid to remain alone on the farm. (Polly, by this time, was living in Johannesburg.)

Within weeks, everyone had forgotten all about Louis Tumpowski. That is, *almost* everyone.

Nearly three months after his mysterious disappearance, Tumpowski's sister, Mrs Saltman who lived in Johannesburg, received a letter from a man who was interested in purchasing the option on *Treurfontein*. He therefore wanted her brother's 'new' address. When Mrs Saltman and her husband Louis made enquires, they became increasingly suspicious. Eventually, she approached the police and asked them to investigate her brother's disappearance.

Mrs Kraft told the police who paid a visit to the farm that she was neither interested in nor concerned about the man's whereabouts. It was her belief, she declared, that Tumpowski had vanished in order to avoid debt repayment. When she heard this explanation, Tumpowski's sister pointed out that it had no basis in truth: her brother's financial affairs had been in perfect order at the time of his disappearance.

About a year was to pass before the police would at last concede to the request made by Tumpowski's sister to conduct a full-scale search of the farm. The investigation was sanctioned by one Inspector A.E. Trigger, head of the Transvaal CID, who had, by this time, come to learn of the option clause in the agreement between Mrs Kraft and Tumpowski, and considered it motive enough for murder. Without a corpse, however, nothing could be proved.

The search was organised by Detective-Sergeant Frederick William Daniels. In July 1920, he began looking for Tumpowski's body on the farm. He used eight prisoners from Lichtenberg Prison to do the digging. For the next month-and-a-half, acres of the farm were dug over, wells were plumbed, and even floors of the farmhouse lifted, but all to no avail. After a month of arduous work, there was no sign of the body and no-one had come forward with information, despite a £100 reward offered by the police.

Daniels had come to hear of Jim Bird during the course of his investigations and on 20 August, went to question him. It was during this interrogation that Bird confessed to taking part in the murder. However, he maintained that because he had run away before the body was disposed of, he had no idea as to the whereabouts of the corpse.

Following this disclosure, Bird joined the eight convicts digging up the farm. At night he was kept in a lock-up because 'there was no other place'.

On 20 September, 1920, almost two-and-a-half years after Tumpowski had been murdered, his body was found by Jim Bird buried on the edge of the ash-pit near the back door of the farmhouse. Although the body was badly decomposed, some grey hair was still visible and there were marks indicating a cut across the throat.

On a finger of the left hand was a signet ring which neighbours were able to identify. A local cobbler also recognized the boots which the corpse was wearing. Louis Tumpowski had finally been found.

The post-mortem showed that Tumpowski had suffered a fractured skull, and there were marks across his throat that indicated knife damage. There was now no doubt that Tumpowski had been murdered.

Shortly afterwards, the police arrested Mrs van der Merwe, Hermanus Swartz, Jim Bird and the three African labourers. At this point, Bird struck a deal with the police, who accepted his offer to turn King's evidence in exchange for immunity from prosecution.

The trial of Mrs van der Merwe began on 13 June, 1921, at the Potchefstroom Circuit Court. Mr Hoal, the State Prosecutor, began his address to the jury by pointing out that, for a guilty verdict to be returned, it was not necessary for the State to prove to the court that Mrs van der Merwe murdered Tumpowski herself, only that she had instigated the crime.

The case for the prosecution hinged on the testimony of Jim Bird, who the judge pointed out was by his own admission a 'liar, adulterer – he had had sexual relations with Mrs Kraft on a number of occasions – witch-doctor and murderer'. Nevertheless, the evidence implicating both Mrs van der Merwe and Mr Swartz in the murder of Tumpowski was so overwhelming that the jury had no hesitation in returning guilty verdicts for both accused.

DECOMPOSITION OF A BODY

…usually begins about 48 hours after death. Roughly 24 hours later, the first visible sign of decomposition is often a greenish discoloration of the abdomen. Around this time too, the veins begin to show through the skin as reddish lines, an effect sometimes known as 'marbling'. After three weeks, the corpse is grossly disfigured: the swollen and bloated features are unrecognizable. The process of liquefaction may have begun.

Moisture and air are essential to the process of decomposition, and tight clothing can 'mummify' a corpse. When exposed to the elements, it normally takes about a year for a corpse to reduce to a skeleton. (Insects and animals may hasten the process, however.) Professor John Glaister, who for many years was Professor of Forensic Medicine at Glasgow University, maintained that, as a general rule, a body decomposes in air twice as quickly as in water, and eight times as rapidly as in earth.

The internal organs decompose at different rates. The brain, stomach and intestines deteriorate quickly, while the lungs, kidneys and uterus take much longer. The elderly tend to decompose more slowly than the young; fat people more quickly than thin ones.

It is interesting to note that some murderers – like Pierre Basson (see Murdering for money*) – have used quicklime in an attempt to hasten the decomposition process. Ironically, under the conditions in which he used it, the substance tends to act as a preservative. Arsenic, too, retards the decomposition process – a tell-tale side-effect of the poison that some murderers have learnt too late.*

Dorothea van der Merwe and Hermanus Swartz were later hanged at Pretoria Central Prison. Two of the African labourers whom Jim Bird claimed had been accessories to the murder of Tumpowski were committed to trial, but later acquitted on lack of evidence. The third man was not tried.

A SHORT HISTORY OF HANGING

Hanging is thought to have originated in Persia (modern Iran) and was brought to Europe in the Middle Ages by the Huns. It was taken to England by the Anglo-Saxons along with other aspects of their culture.

Originally, criminals were simply strung-up from the branch of a tree. The first innovation to this practice was the construction of rudimentary gallows – normally two legs supporting a cross-beam. The condemned person mounted a ladder placed against the cross-beam, had a noose put around his or her neck, and the ladder pushed away. This form of execution normally resulted in slow strangulation and spectators were often in the habit of pulling on the victim's legs to hasten the end.

In the latter half of the eighteenth century, the first 'modern' gallows, designed to fracture the victim's neck, was introduced. This device made use of a properly constructed noose which was positioned under the chin in order to fracture the cervical vertebrae, and a trap-door through which the victim fell when a lever was pulled.

In the second quarter of the nineteenth century there was an attempt to make hangings more 'humane'. In England, public executions ceased and prisoners were no longer left hanging on the gibbet to rot. The famous Yorkshire executioner, James Berry, also devised a Table of Drops based upon the weight of the prisoner and the length of the fall required to kill him. The object of this table was to ensure that the victim died instantaneously and with as few marks as possible. (If the rope was too short, prisoners tended to die of strangulation, and if the rope was too long, it literally tore the victim's head off.)

Death from hanging under properly supervised control is normally instantaneous, although heart and lung action may continue for up to fifteen minutes. The victim is normally left to hang after execution for approximately one hour to ensure death. In less civilised times, burial alive was a very real possibility!

4.

BLOOD FOR BLOOD

(STEPHANUS SWART, 1927)

In the final stop-press edition of the Johannesburg *Star* on Friday, 6 May, 1927, the following news story appeared:

> **NINE KILLED IN SHOOTING TRAGEDY**
> **NATAL BORDER SENSATION**
> **EARLY MORNING FIGHT WITH POLICE**
>
> *A well-known farmer in the Charlestown district named S.A.J. Swart, this morning ran amok and killed 8 Europeans and a native, wounded 3 other Europeans and then shot himself. Among those killed was his wife and the officer commanding the posse of police who went to arrest Swart.*

Stephanus Swart had always been a violent, unpredictable man. For a number of years he had displayed some of the classic symptoms of paranoid schizophrenia – extreme mood swings, hostility towards authority, and feelings of persecution – but no one could have predicted the course of events that would take place that fine autumn morning.

Swart was wedded to a woman thirty years his senior. Many people in the district believed he had married the widow for her money – her first husband, Eksteen, had left her a number of farms. Certainly, the union appeared loveless, and Swart was resented by some of his in-laws.

He was a poorly educated man, but there was one thing he had learned in his thirty-seven years, and that was that he would find no justice in the courts.

Perhaps this belief had its beginnings some years earlier, when Swart lost a civil suit. He felt, as he would make clear to anyone who would listen, that he had been not only unfairly treated on that occasion, but actually victimized. The evidence indicated quite the reverse. Nevertheless, Swart grew increasingly embittered with age, and his temper, rather than mellowing, deterioriated.

In a second and much more serious incident a few years after the civil suit, Swart viciously assaulted a relative and was sentenced to imprisonment for eighteen months. As far as Swart was concerned, the judge had handed down this harsh sentence purely out of personal animosity. It was confirmation of his worst fears: that the authorities were against him. He determined that in future he would solve his own problems in his own way.

On his release from prison, Swart returned to his wife, from whom he was judicially separated, who was living at *Potter's Hill*. The farm belonged to Mrs Knight, Mrs Swart's daughter by her first marriage.

Early in 1927, Swart was accused of committing 'a serious sexual offence', namely incest. He had some difficulty raising the £500 bail required, having ignored the suggestion from many quarters that he sell some of his livestock to make the money, because he felt it would have been unfair on the animals. (He knew he could trust no-one but himself to care for them properly.) The hearing was set for 4 May.

Now, in the knowledge that he would certainly face a long prison term if he should be found guilty, and with the trial only two months off, Swart had to deal with the next problem. Both his wife, and his stepdaughter's farm manager, Mr J.C. Visser, had been called as witnesses against him.

Swart solved this complication in a simple and direct way: he threatened to kill them if they attempted to speak against him. Visser, who had managed the farm for nine months, and Mrs Swart both knew that Stephanus meant what he said, and they promised to keep quiet about the whole business. Visser even said that he would go to Worcester in the Cape to avoid being subpoenaed by the police. True to his word, he left the farm a few days later. Soon after, Mrs Swart left for Potchefstroom. She knew that her husband was having an affair with a young girl and, like Visser, she had every intention of giving evidence at his trial.

Swart was obviously under a great deal of strain at this time. Towards the end of April 1927, he was fined 10 s by a local magistrate for driving an unlicensed vehicle. This seemingly unimportant episode may have been the last straw for Swart. On Tuesday, 3 May, the day before he was due to appear in the Magistrates' Court, he drove over to a neighbouring farm and, for no apparent reason, fired a shot at the owner of the farm, a Mr Lourens. He had begun to lose control.

When the police learnt of Swart's unprovoked attack, they issued a warrant of arrest for attempted murder. The final act in his tragic drama was about to be played out.

Accordingly, Swart made careful preparations for the grand finale.

He began by summoning his attorney, Mr G. Maasdorp, to *Potter's Hill*. He wished, he said, to put his personal affairs in order.

This kind of behaviour is not uncommon among aggressive psychopaths. Such people have been known to commit crimes of violence with careful premeditation and planning, and a lack of compassion that even close friends and family find hard to understand. Psychologists believe that an unbalanced emotional state is the cause of psychopathic hostility, which takes the form of remoteness and seeming indifference to the plight of others.

Before Maasdorp set out for *Potter's Hill*, he contacted the local police commander, Captain Gerald Ashman, and asked him whether he should delay seeing his client until after Swart's arrest. Captain Ashman suggested to Maasdorp that he go to *Potter's Hill* in order to try to persuade Swart to give himself up. Accordingly, Mr Maasdorp hired Mr B. Plaats as driver and, in the late afternoon of Wednesday, 4 May, the two men set out for the farm.

Swart turned out to be intractable. For five days he had roamed the farm planning his revenge, driving himself and his farm labourers to the point of exhaustion in the process. At night, he had locked himself in the farmhouse and sat with his gun primed, raging against the authorities. Maasdorp was convinced that the man was mentally disturbed.

He learnt that Swart had gone to Potchefstroom a few days before in order to see his wife and reiterate his threat – only to learn that she had left for Newcastle. He followed her there, but was unable to find her. On his way home, Swart claimed that he had suddenly realised that if something were to happen to him his car would fall into the hands of his enemies. He had to prevent this from occurring at all costs, so he stopped at the side of the road, set the car alight, and walked the last ten miles to his home.

Swart refused to listen to reason and Maasdorp was forced to listen to his ravings until late into the night. In the end, he ordered Maasdorp to write down a statement. This last testament to the madness of Stephanus Swart was twenty-eight pages long and contained the following excerpt:

> *I have arranged all my affairs with my attorney. I now give blood for blood. I will shoot them down till I have one cartridge left. And that will be mine. But alive you will never get me. With my corpse you can do what you please. Burn it, mutilate it and treat it in such a manner as you think fit to best revenge yourselves. I wish this statement to be published after my death in all the prominent newspapers in the Union and I desire a copy to be forwarded to the Prime Minister, General Hertzog.*

When Captain Ashman heard of Swart's ravings the following day, he was greatly concerned. He knew Swart to be a crack shot (everyone in the district knew that) and a man who was more than capable of carrying out his threats. In an effort to defuse what was quickly becoming an extremely volatile situation, Ashman asked Mr Plaats to return to *Potter's Hill* with a message for Swart. In this note, he advised the farmer to give himself up. In this way, he said, a great deal of unnecessary trouble could be avoided.

He also offered to meet with Swart alone to discuss the matter.

Courting detection and punishment was also behaviour typical of a psychopathic disposition. Many of the world's most notorious killers, particularly those who commit sexual crimes, have apparently craved the attention their deeds have brought them. Neville Heath was a case in point. Labelled 'the most sadistic sex killer of all time' during his trial at London's Old Bailey in 1946, Heath had so enjoyed the limelight that he had approached the police in order to see a photograph of the woman he had murdered.

Swart seemed in a much calmer mood when Plaats returned to the farm. He listened quietly while the letter was read out to him, then gave his reply.

He was prepared to meet with Captains Ashman and Maasdorp if the two men arrived at his farm before sunset. However, at 6.00 p.m., he said, he intended to close the main road that ran through his property and shoot on sight anyone who attempted to cross his land. Then he gave his final instruction to Plaats: he wished to have a coffin ordered in Volksrust. The casket was to be made of oak and to be zinc-lined, and it should not cost more than £40.

When Ashman heard Swart's reply, he knew that the time for talking was over. He gathered together a detail of 12 policemen and before dawn on Friday, 6 May, they set out in two cars and a motorcycle-with-sidecar on the fourteen-mile journey from the Charlestown Hotel to *Potter's Hill*.

The police convoy halted at the boundary of Swart's property. The policemen disembarked and split into three groups. The plan was for Captain Ashman and his second-in-command, Sergeant Annes van Wyk, to direct operations from a small Indian trading store on the boundary of Swart's property, while the other two groups advanced on the farmhouse from different directions. One party would move in from below and the other from a point higher up the hillside. However, just as the men were about to set out, one of Swart's farm labourers galloped out of the early morning mist with a warning that Swart was preparing to fight them.

Captain Ashman listened to the man, then gave some last instructions: he wanted Swart taken alive if possible.

What the police did not realise was that Swart had gone on the offensive. He had left the farmhouse and moved out into the fields.

The first casualty was Constable Feucht, who was shot as he approached the farmhouse. In a great deal of pain, he made his way back to Captain Ashman, who sent him back to the town for medical attention. At this point, Ashman sent a note to Sergeant Watts, who was leading the uphill party:

Carefully take cover towards house and shoot Swart on sight. Feucht wounded with shotgun and gone to hospital. Have sent for more men. Try to save yourselves and do not expose, as Swart is now desperate.

Shortly after this, Swart shot and killed two more policemen – Sergeant William Charles Mitchell and Constable William Crossman. After bringing down the men he had shot both of them at point-blank range to make certain they were dead.

By this time, Swart had realised that, despite his success in having killed three policemen, he would ultimately be captured. He had other tasks he had to complete first. With the police closing in, he decided to make use of the thick mist to effect his escape across a mealie patch. It was while making this manoeuvre that he encountered his fourth victim, Sergeant Grove. Mortally wounded, Grove died from loss of blood after crawling hundreds of metres.

After killing Sergeant Grove, Swart planned to make good his escape, but not before paying a visit to Captain Ashman and Sergeant Van Wyk in order to seize the horse which his labourer had been riding when he first galloped out of the mist. Swart shot both men dead. Then, before setting out for Charlestown, where his wife was living, he took Captain Ashman's Webley service revolver to add to the Mauser rifle and Browning automatic pistol he was already carrying.

En route to Charlestown, Swart stopped for a cup of coffee at his neighbour's farm. By this time it was eight o'clock and the day was brightening. He seemed in the best of spirits.

'I've just killed five policemen,' he boasted, 'and now I'm going to Charlestown to shoot three more people. If I get through that alive I'm heading for Volkrust where I intend to kill myself.' To substantiate his story, he produced Captain Ashman's Webley.

Swanepoel listened in silent astonishment then, the moment Swart had departed, saddled his own horse and set out to warn the police that Swart was on his way. He was nearing Mount Prospect when an African rode up and handed him a note from Swart. In it, Swart promised to return and kill Swanepoel when he had completed his mission. This was shortly after he had killed two more people on the road – Mrs Knight and Mr M. Roets (who was farm manager for Mr Lourens), both of whom had recently given evidence against him.

Mrs Swart was staying with the Van Vuuren family, who lived about three-hundred metres from the Charlestown railway station. When Swart galloped up to the house, Mrs Swart, 17-year-old Gertrude van Vuuren, and Lucas, her crippled, 21-year-old cousin, were sitting on the stoep.

Even from a distance, Gertrude was frightened by the look on Swart's face. She called to her sister and together the two girls rushed nextdoor. Their neighbour, Mrs Thomas, seemed to know instinctively that disaster was at hand.

'Run to the police station,' she shouted. The girls ran out of Mrs Thomas' yard just as two shots were fired. Behind them, Swart had walked calmly into the house and shot his wife twice, once in the forehead and once in the chest.

Gertrude and her sister, along with two other women, Mrs Grove and Mrs Erasmus, locked themselves in the police station and prayed that help would come. Two hours passed before a constable came to release them from their ordeal.

After killing his wife, Swart rode to the edge of town. At the main road, he tethered his exhausted horse to a fence. He tried to wave down the first car that came along. Inside were Mrs Pulford, wife of the manager of the Charlestown and District Co-operative Stores; Mr Hadley, a local farmer; and his three year-old nephew. When Mr Hadley failed to stop, Swart fired at the car. Both Hadley and Mrs Pulford were wounded, but they managed to drive on to safety.

By this time, the whole district was getting to know of Swart's reign of terror. The police and local farmers were mobilized to hunt him down, and a posse eventually caught up with him near Johannes Swanepoel's farm.

Spotting Swart in the distance, the station foreman at Charlestown, a man named Kriel, fired three shots in rapid succession. Swart dived into the *veld* at the side of the road just as a contingent of regular police from Volksrust arrived on the scene. Seconds later, a fourth shot rang out.

In what was perhaps Swart's final act of defiance of authority, he had shot himself in the head with Captain Ashman's Webley. He had indeed done as he had promised: returned blood for blood.

5.

'THE MOST DASTARDLY CRIME IN THE CALENDAR'

(PETRUS STEPHANUS HAUPTFLEISCH: 1925)

Matricide is a relatively rare crime. There is evidence to suggest that, in most instances, the killer is excessively attached to his or her mother and the act of murder is a demonstration of independence.

However, Petrus Stephanus Francois Hauptfleisch, who murdered his mother on Tuesday, 13 January, 1925, appears to have been been motivated, at least in part, by greed.

Until he was over thirty, Hauptfleisch lived with his mother at Richmond in the Cape. Shortly after the outbreak of World War I, he gave up the property he had been farming and volunteered for the army. He entered active service and for four years fought in the trenches of Europe.

He returned to Richmond in 1919. By 1925, he was married and had a young child, but his constant drinking and violent temper drove his wife to leave him. After the break-up of his marriage, Hauptfleisch went to live with his widowed mother, Barbara, at her house on the outskirts of the town.

At first, Hauptfleisch worked at a local butchery, then he set himself up slaughtering animals on his own. His drinking problem grew so bad that eventually neither the bottle stores nor the hotels in the town would sell him liquor.

Early in December 1924, this drinking ban was temporarily rescinded. Hauptfleisch responded by taking to the bottle once more. On the night of 11 December, he became drunk and aggressive. His mother was so afraid for her own safety that she ran to a neighbour's house.

'Petrus says he's going to stone me to death,' she said. Pointing to a pile of stones lying in the garden, she continued, 'He was so angry he threw them on the roof of the house.' Her neighbour, Mr Pieter Theron, was alarmed enough to call the police.

When Constable Strydom arrived, Hauptfleisch was still aggressive. 'Surely you don't believe that old woman?' he shouted. 'She's off her head!' But Constable Strydom was not that easily put off. He arrested Hauptfleisch and locked him up in the police station for the night. By the next morning, Hauptfleisch had sobered up, but he remained bitterly resentful of his mother. When he became drunk again two days later, he was once again blacklisted by Richmond's liquor outlets, this time at the insistence of his mother. It seems that, as far as Hauptfleisch was concerned, this was the final insult. He was left with no alternative but to get rid of her. Just two days later, he began to make preparations.

Mrs Hauptfleisch was last seen alive at around 2 p.m. on the afternoon of 13 January, 1925, when her next-door neighbour, Mrs Christina Botes, spoke to her over the back garden fence. Just after three o'clock, Petrus Hauptfleisch strolled along to the Botes' home and chátted to Joanna, Mrs Botes' twenty year-old daughter, who was sewing on the front stoep. Ten minutes later Petrus visited Mrs Jacoba Nieuwoudt who lived directly across the street. Mrs Nieuwoudt invited him into the house, but he declined, saying that he was on his way to the shops to buy sugar for his mother.

At around twenty minutes to four Petrus arrived at Barend Pienaar's store. He was in the habit of going there most days to read the newspaper for about half an hour. This particular afternoon was no exception. Petrus left the shop just after 4 p.m. and was not seen for the next hour. He would later claim that he had spent this time scouring the koppies outside the town in search of a blind Swiss goat and kid that he had lost. After a long search, he had found the two animals, and had taken them to the town's showground.

He then went to Conradie's general store, where he bought the sugar his mother needed, and some cigarettes for himself. After spending some time chatting to the owner, Hauptfleisch walked home in the company of Mr Hendrik Victor. He reached his mother's house at about 5.45 p.m.. He was later to claim that he had been out of the house between 3.00 and 5.45 p.m..

This version of events was contradicted to some extent by Petrus Booysen, the superintendent of the Indigent Boarding House in Richmond. Booysen saw Hauptfleisch outside his mother's house at exactly two minutes to five. (He was able to fix the time accurately because two minutes after they had passed each other in the street the church clock struck five.)

Hauptfleisch had been in the house only a few seconds when he ran out into the street again. 'Oh, God, help!' he screamed, and dashed across to Mrs Nieuwoudt's house. 'My mother's been burnt,' he shouted, then rushed home again. Mrs Botes, the next-door neighbour, had also heard the commotion. Thinking that Mrs Hauptfleisch had been taken ill, she ran quickly to the house and followed Petrus inside.

Mrs Hauptfleisch was dead in the kitchen. She was lying half-naked on her right side on the raised stone hearth. Her head, which was resting on a pile of ash in the fireplace, was directly beneath the chimney. Although there was no fire in the grate, her right side was badly burnt.

Petrus tenderly lifted his mother from the fireplace and placed her body on a small kitchen stool, propping her elbows up on the hearth. Then he left Mrs Botes and some of the other neighbours who had been drawn by the commotion, and ran to notify the police. He went to the house of Sergeant Brooks. While Brooks set about informing the local magistrate, Mr R.W. Lambert, and the District Surgeon, Dr J.H. Bam, he sent Constable J.C. Blom back to the house with Hauptfleisch.

As soon as they arrived, Constable Blom ordered everyone out of the house while he made a preliminary examination of the scene. He noted fragments of burnt clothing on the floor and a cork on a nearby table. There was a small pile of ash in the grate, within which was an indentation where Mrs Hauptfleisch's head had rested. The ash also contained a burnt matchbox, matches and several fragments of broken glass. There was no fire in the stove, and in the oven was a cold plate of cooked liver.

Shortly afterwards, Dr Bam arrived. Mrs Hauptfleisch's death had surprised him. He knew she was nearing 70, but she had always been a vigorous, active woman and, as far as he was concerned, she had been in the best of health.

Noting that her hands were semi-clenched, which was unusual in a death of this sort, he asked, 'Is this how you found her, Petrus?'

Hauptfleisch shook his head. 'No. She was lying in the hearth with her face in the fire. I think she was trying to "burn out" the chimney with petrol,' he said.

Using petrol to clean soot from the chimney was a dangerous job – not at all the sort of thing Dr Bam would have expected from Mrs Hauptfleisch. Moreover, when he glanced up the chimney, it appeared clean.

When Dr Bam began to examine Mrs Hauptfleisch's body, he felt stirrings of alarm. At first glance, the damage seemed entirely consistent with Petrus's account of the accident – the hair on the left side of her head was charred and there were burns on her upper body, left arm, face and neck – but all

POST-MORTEM LIVIDITY – also referred to as hypostasis or livor mortis – is the process whereby blood drains to the lowest parts of the corpse as the result of gravity. There it collects and coagulates in the vessels, causing livid patches or staining on the skin. Lividity begins immediately after death, but the associated dark patches on the skin do not normally show for three to four hours. They are fully evident after twelve hours. However, lividity patches never occur at those points where the body has been in direct contact with a hard surface or where the bloodflow has been restricted by tight clothing.

the post-mortem lividity patches he observed on her body were in the wrong places.

In this case, these stained patches showed on the back of Mrs Hautpfleisch's corpse, in the lumbar region and on her heels. If she had died lying face-down in the hearth, as Petrus claimed, they would have been on the front parts of her body. The lividity patches on Mrs Hauptfleisch's body therefore indicated that she had died on her *back*!

At ten o'clock the following morning, Dr Bam conducted a post-mortem on Mrs Hauptfleisch and discovered that she had neither burnt to death nor suffered a 'heart spasm' as her son had suggested. She had suffocated.

Dr Bám based his conclusion on a number of facts. Firstly, there were no traces of soot or carbon either in the old lady's windpipe or in her brochial tubes, indicating that she had not died in a fire. Secondly, her lungs were dark-coloured, engorged with blood, and full of air. This suggested that she had not died instantaneously. Thirdly, her blood was black and fluid (uncoagulated) – both indications of asphyxia.

Dr Bam also found evidence of internal haemorrhage in Mrs Hauptfleisch's lower stomach, a type of injury which is usually caused by a sharp blow or heavy pressure to the area in question, but he could only surmise as to the cause of this injury.

Despite Dr Bam's conviction that Mrs Hauptfleisch had been murdered, he was not able to state with absolute certainty that there had been foul play, because the victim's neck and throat had been too badly charred for any strangulation marks to show. However, Dr Bam was later able to conclude, 'From my examination I could come to only one diagnosis, and that was that the woman had died of suffocation.'

Shortly after Mrs Hauptfleisch's post-mortem, Petrus was arrested and charged with her murder. It was believed that his motive for the crime was simple greed: he was the sole benefactor named in his mother's will, and he stood to inherit over £600.

Petrus Hauptfleisch's trial, which was held at the Supreme Court in Cape Town, began on Monday, 21 September, 1925.

The Crown, which based its case essentially on the overwhelming volume of circumstantial evidence which linked Hauptfleisch to the death of his mother, contended that Mrs Hauptfleisch had retired to bed for a nap at about 3 p.m. on the afternoon of her death, and that her son had crept into the room and suffocated her, probably with a pillow. (The internal haemorrhage noted by Dr Bam would have been caused by his kneeling on her stomach to apply the pressure. The ensuing struggle would also explain her clenched hands.) Furthermore, Mrs S. van Niekerk, who had entered the house shortly after the body had been discovered, had noticed that Mrs Hauptfleisch's bed had been 'slept in' when she went to get a blanket to cover the body.

The Crown further contended that Hauptfleisch had wandered around the town in order to establish an alibi, then had returned to the house at around 4 p.m., carried his mother's body into the kitchen, and contrived the 'accidental death' scene. Unfortunately for him, he had been seen in the vicinity of the house just before 5 p.m. by Mr Booysen.

What was more, a few days before the death he had sent a fourteen year-old schoolboy, named Daniel van Niekerk, to buy a sixpence-worth of petrol, yet on the afternoon of the accident, he had told Dr Bam that he did not know where the petrol was.

Another witness, Mr Conradie, claimed that, when he had asked Hauptfleisch what had caused his mother's death, he had replied that 'she had been speaking for some days of burning out the chimney with petrol'. Conradie later remarked that he had never heard of anyone doing such a thing before.

On Friday, 25 September, Petrus Hauptfleisch was found guilty of murder. The judge, Justice van Zyl, turned to the accused before he passed sentence. 'Is there anything you wish to say to the court?' he asked.

For a moment or two, Hauptfleisch nervously stroked his chin and clasped and unclasped his hands; then, as if pulling himself together, he began to speak in a clear, low voice.

'My Lord and gentlemen of the jury. In this matter my learned counsel has already pointed out to you the most important facts. I really cannot say anything to supplement his address. But as this opportunity is afforded me, I would like to say something about the effect my prosecution has had on me personally.

'The crime with which I have been charged, matricide, is one I consider the most dastardly in the calendar. It is for me inconceivable that any man with ordinary intelligence, unless he be mentally deranged, could stoop to take the life of one who conceived his existence, nursed it and gave him life. It is a crime for which I have had great abhorrence since my puberty. That, in itself, is sufficient to justify my innocence. The very fact that I have even been suspected of murdering my mother, coupled with this prosecution, has during many months of awaiting trial – about eight months in all – caused me incomprehensible agony and, had I been guilty of the commission of this crime, I would gladly and voluntarily have made my confession to gain the punishment which would have terminated my agonized existence.

'I was an only son, an only child. I was spoiled and the result was bad company. All these facts, combined, strongly stimulated by extraneous influences, turned me out other than the dutiful son my mother expected. I have no compunction in acknowledging these facts. For although I am disgraced by being suspected even of such a crime, I cannot do otherwise in duty to my wife and child. Although it is a further humiliation, I cannot remain silent.

'I think, in analysing the various depositions, that the element of possibility of the crime is only apparent, while the rest is merely circumstantial. Such being the case, there is a doubt. I know there is a doubt. No man is convicted of a crime unless he is conclusively proved guilty. And I humbly submit that the evidence tendered by the Crown is too unfounded, too slender, too doubtful to justify a conviction. In conclusion, my Lord and gentlemen of the jury, I humbly commit myself to the clemency of the court, knowing full well that I shall receive the degree of justice and mercy that I so humbly and urgently solicit.'

He paused, then added, 'It is not only punishing me, my Lord, an innocent man. I am now condemned. It is not only I who am punished, but my innocent wife and child as well. They too must suffer.'

'Is that all you wish to say?' Justice van Zyl asked.

'Yes, thank you, my Lord,' Hauptfleisch responded.

'Then I have no further discretion in the matter.'

So saying, he passed sentence of death on Hauptfleisch.

The convicted man spent 83 days in the condemned cell, during which time the body of his mother was exhumed for further investigation. However, the patholgist who conducted the autopsy could find no reason to argue with the State. On 18 December, 1925, Petrus Stephanus Francois Hauptfleisch was informed that all his appeals had been turned down. Five days later, at seven o'clock in the morning on 23 December, 1925, he was hanged. He went to his death protesting his innocence.

6.

SOUTH AFRICA'S MOST FAMOUS POISONER

(DAISY DE MELKER: 1932)

On 17 October, 1932, at Johannesburg High Court, there began the trial of Daisy Louisa de Melker, who was charged with the murder of two husbands and her twenty year-old son, Rhodes.

The case attracted almost unprecedented public interest. Queues of spectators lined up for hours each day before the proceedings began. On the final day of the trial, some spectators who had waited overnight to ensure a place in the court sold their seats for up to 30 s each!

At that time it was normal for anyone accused of murder under South African law to be tried by a judge and jury, although the law allowed them the option of being tried by a judge and two assessors. Since public opinion weighed so heavily against Mrs de Melker, she had opted, on the advice of her legal counsel, for the latter.

The proceedings were opened before Mr Justice Greenberg and two senior magistrates, Mr J.M. Graham and Mr A.A. Stanford. Mrs de Melker faced three charges. Firstly that, on or about 11 January, 1923, and at or near Bertrams, in the district of Johannesburg, she had murdered her husband, William Alfred Cowle, by poisoning him with strychnine. Secondly, that on or about 6 November, 1927, in the same district, she had murdered her second husband, Robert Sproat, by poisoning him with strychnine and, thirdly, that upon or about 5 March, 1932, in the district of Germiston, she had murdered her son, Rhodes Cecil Cowle, by administering him poison, namely arsenic.

Daisy de Melker (*nee* Hancorn-Smith) was born on 1 June, 1886, at Seven Fountains near Grahamstown. She was one of eleven children. When she was twelve, she went to Bulawayo to live with her father and two of her brothers. Three years later, she became a boarder at the Good Hope Seminary School in Cape Town. She returned to Rhodesia (as it then was) in 1903, but apparently found rural life unexciting, because it was not long before she returned to South Africa and enrolled at the Berea Nursing Home in Durban. On one of her holidays in Rhodesia, she met and fell in love with a young man named Bert Fuller who was a civil servant in the Native Affairs Department at Broken Hill. They planned to marry in October, 1907.

However, Fuller contracted black-water fever and died, with Daisy at his bedside, on the very day they had planned to marry. Fuller left a will bequeathing £100 to his fiance.

In March 1909, about eighteen months after the death of Bert Fuller, Daisy Hancorn-Smith married William Alfred Cowle, a plumber, in Johannesburg. She was 23; he was 36.

The couple had five children, four of whom died. The first were twins, who died in infancy; their third child died of an abscess on the liver; and the fourth suffered convulsions and bowel trouble and died at the age of 15 months. Their last, and only surviving child, Rhodes Cecil, was born in June 1911.

Early on the morning of 11 January, 1923, William Cowle became ill soon after taking Epsom salts prepared by his wife. The first doctor who attended him did not consider his condition serious and prescribed a bromide mixture. But, Cowle's condition deteriorated rapidly. Not long after the doctor had left, he took a turn for the worse. His wife summoned the neighbours to help and called for another doctor.

Cowle was in excruciating pain when the second doctor arrived. He foamed at the mouth, was blue in the face, and screamed in agony if anyone touched him until he died.

STRYCHNINE is a colourless, crystalline powder with an exceptionally bitter taste. It is obtained from Strychos nux vomica *and other plants.*

About one-and-a-half grains (100 milligrams) constitutes a fatal dose, although 15 mg of the poison has proved fatal, and toxic symptoms can result from a dose as small as 5 mg.

Strychnine poisoning causes the muscles of the back to go into spasm, causing convulsions so intense that the body arches violently. This symptom, called opisthotonus, *can last for up to two minutes, during which time the victim is conscious and in extreme pain. Sometimes the muscles of the face are drawn up in a horrifying 'smile of death' (referred to as the* risus sardonicus *in some older textbooks). Eventually, these muscular tensions prevent the lungs from working. Death, either from respiratory failure or exhaustion, usually follows within an hour.*

In the past, strychnine has been used as a rat poison. At one time, there was also a plethora of strychnine-based 'tonics' available. These were usually prescribed to invalids and people recovering from a long illness. Tiny amounts of the drug have the effect of raising the blood pressure slightly, which tends to create a general feeling of well-being. Not surprisingly, accidental deaths (and suicides) from strychnine poisoning were fairly common. These would result if the bottle had not been shaken properly: the patient would take a dose of the concentrated liquid which had accumulated at the bottom.

Faced with these symptoms, the second doctor suspected strychnine poisoning and refused to sign the death certificate. A post-mortem was subsequently performed by the acting District Surgeon, Dr Fergus. The cause of death was certified to be chronic nephritis and cerebal haemorrhage.

Daisy Cowle, the sole beneficiary of her husband's will, inherited £1 795.

At the age of thirty-six, and three years to the day after the death of her first husband, Daisy Cowle married another plumber. His name was Robert Sproat, and he was ten years her senior.

In October 1927, Robert Sproat became violently ill. He was in great agony and suffered severe muscle spasms similar to those experienced by William Cowle. He recovered. A few weeks later, he suffered a second, fatal attack after drinking some beer in the company of his wife and stepson, Rhodes. He died on 6 November, 1927. Dr Mallinick, the attending physician, certified that the cause of death was arteriosclerosis and cerebral haemorrhage. No autopsy was performed.

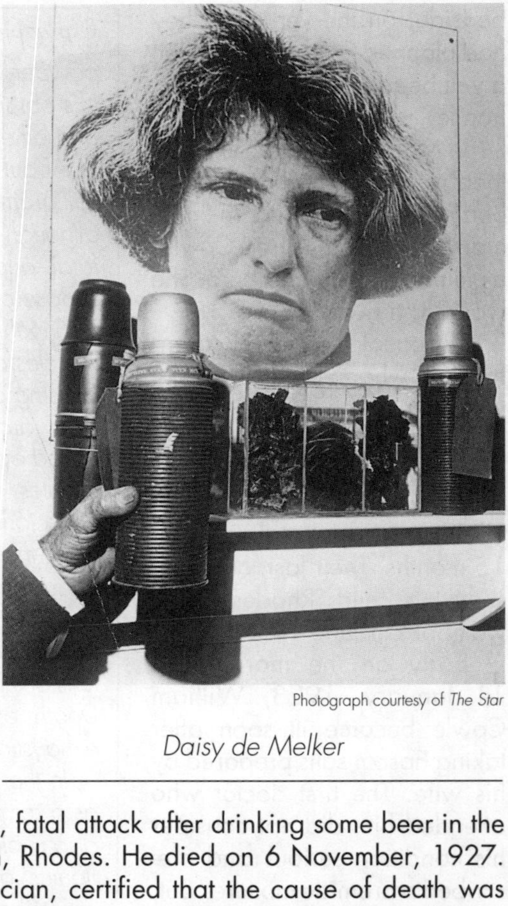

Photograph courtesy of *The Star*

Daisy de Melker

Following Robert Sproat's death, his widow inherited over £4 000, plus a further £560 paid by his pension fund.

On 21 January, 1931, Daisy Sproat married for the third time. Her husband was a widower, Sydney Clarence de Melker, who, like her previous two husbands, was a plumber.

By this time, Rhodes Cowle was nineteen. His sister-in-law, Eileen de Melker, thought him lazy and remarked that he was often unwilling to get up for work in the morning. However, another witness at his mother's trial described him as 'bright and conscientious'. A girl who had met Rhodes at a party a few weeks before his death maintained that he was 'a real gentleman'. Certainly, the evidence conflicted, but none of it explained why Daisy de Melker decided to

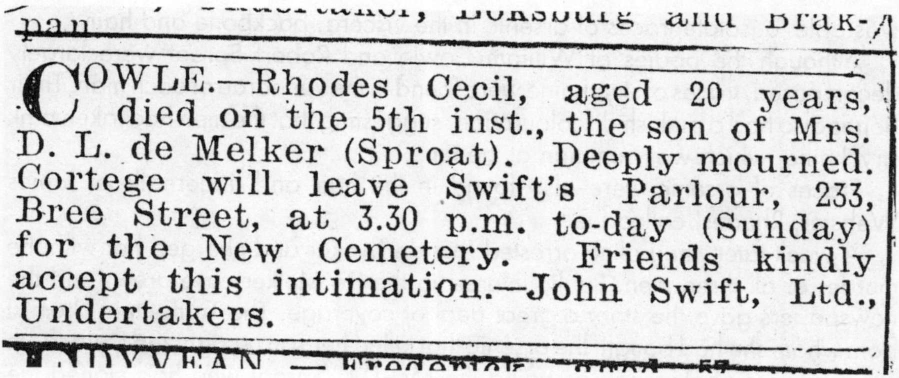
Undertaker, Boksburg and Brak-pan

COWLE.—Rhodes Cecil, aged 20 years, died on the 5th inst., the son of Mrs. D. L. de Melker (Sproat). Deeply mourned. Cortege will leave Swift's Parlour, 233, Bree Street, at 3.30 p.m. to-day (Sunday) for the New Cemetery. Friends kindly accept this intimation.—John Swift, Ltd., Undertakers.

kill Rhodes. In the case of her first two husbands, the motive seemed clearly to be financial gain. But why kill her son?

Rhodes seems to have been under the impression that he would come into an inheritance at the age of 21. Perhaps he was demanding more than she could give him and was becoming a burden to her? The most obvious answer is that she simply didn't like him. He was a disappointment to her. She had pampered him all his life, but he rarely showed her any consideration in return.

Whatever the cause, late in February 1932, Mrs de Melker travelled many kilometres, from Germiston to Turffontein, to obtain a quantity of arsenic from a chemist there. She used her former name, Sproat, and claimed that she required the poison to destroy a sick cat.

Less than a week later, on Wednesday, 2 March, 1927, Rhodes took ill at work after drinking coffee from a thermos flask which his mother had prepared for him. A fellow worker, James Webster, also became violently sick. Webster, who had drunk very little of the coffee, recovered within a few days, but Rhodes died at home at midday on the following Saturday.

A post-mortem followed and the cause of death was given as cerebral malaria. Rhodes was buried at New Brixton cemetery the following day.

On 1 April, Mrs de Melker received £100 from Rhodes' life insurance policy. But the story doesn't end there, of course.

By this time, William Sproat, her dead husband's brother, had become suspicious. Eventually these suspicions were conveyed to the authorities and, on 15 April, the police obtained a court order permitting them to exhume the bodies of Rhodes Cowle, Robert Sproat and William Cowle.

The first body to be removed was that of Rhodes Cowle. The corpse was found to be in an unusually good state of preservation – which is characteristic of the presence of arsenic in large quantities. Sure enough, the government analyst was able to isolate traces of arsenic in the viscera, backbone and hair.

Although the bodies of William Cowle and Robert Sproat were largely decomposed, traces of strychnine were found in the vertebrae of each man. Their bones also had a pinkish discolouration, suggesting that the men had taken pink strychnine, which was common at the time.

Traces of arsenic were also found in the hair and fingernails of James Webster, Rhodes' colleague.

A week later, the police arrested Mrs de Melker and charged her with the murder of all three men. Public interest in the De Melker case grew, and the newspapers gave the story a great deal of coverage. The Turffontein chemist from whom she had bought the arsenic that killed her son recognized Daisy from a newspaper photograph as being the Mrs D.L. Sproat who had signed the poisons register and went to the police.

The De Melker trial lasted thirty days. Sixty witnesses were called for the Crown and less than half this number for the defence. To present the forensic evidence, the Crown employed the services of Dr J.M. Watt, an expert toxicologist and Professor of Pharmacology at the Witwatersrand University.

In summing up, before giving his verdict, the judge pointed out that the State had been unable to prove conclusively that Cowle and Sproat had died of strychnine poisoning. 'It does not convince me, nor does it convict the accused,' he said.

On the third count, however, he had come to the 'inescapable conclusion' that Mrs de Melker had murdered her son. This was evident because:

(a) Rhodes Cowle had died of arsenic poisoning;
(b) the coffee flask held traces of arsenic;
(c) the accused had put the arsenic into the flask ('I can see no escape from the conclusion that the accused put arsenic into the flask...') on the Wednesday prior to Rhodes Cowle's death; and
(d) the defence of suicide was untenable.

When the judge finally turned to pass sentence on Mrs de Melker, her face whitened, and for a moment all the strength seemed to leave her body.

'You have been found guilty of the murder of your son, Rhodes Cecil Cowle. Do you have anything to say before I pass sentence of death on you?'

A hushed silence fell over the court.

'I am not guilty of poisoning my son.'

'There is only one sentence I can pass,' responded the judge, and, so saying, he condemned her to death by hanging.

On the morning of 30 December, 1932, Daisy de Melker was hanged.

7.

THE WOMAN WHO TALKED HER WAY TO THE GALLOWS

(MARIA HELENA GERTRUIDA LEE: 1947)

Between October 1946 and May 1947, Maria Lee used arsenic to poison to death her young lover, Alwyn Smith, a man she claimed ardently to love.

Maria Helena Gertruida Lee (*nee* Van Niekerk) was born in 1899. When she met Alwyn Smith in 1945, she was 46 and had been married three times. He was twenty-six.

Her first husband was named Oosterhuizen. They were married in 1915 and lived in the Lichtenburg district where they raised four sons. In 1929, the couple divorced.

She remarried soon afterwards, but her second marriage to a man named Kruger lasted only a few short months.

On 1 December, 1934, she married Jan de Klerk Lee, a twenty-four year-old metal worker. She sold the tea-room she had been running in Johannesburg and they set up home together in Pretoria. She began buying sites, building houses, and then selling them. Just seven months later, in March 1941, Lee went into hospital suffering from tuberculosis. He died in July of the same year and Mrs Lee inherited close to £3 000 from her husband's estate.

After three marriages, Mrs Lee was well set up: she was a wealthy and attractive widow in her early forties. However, she had an insatiable appetite for young male friends, and it was this fatal attraction which was, in the end, to lead to her downfall.

Soon after Jan Lee's death, she was engaged again, this time to one of her husband's friends. But, when she found out that the man was suffering from a serious illness, she broke off the relationship and made the decision to move to the Cape. In 1945, she applied for a job with Lennons – a pharmaceutical firm in Cape Town. In her letter of application, she maintained she was a twenty-nine year-old widow, with no children, whose husband had been killed in the North African campaign.

'The whole letter was nonsense,' she would later explain at her trial. 'But I had to do it for a reason... It was a disease which might have ended in death or have resulted in long suffering. I could not face death again and would have done anything to break it off. I then wrote to Lennons. I had to go to any place where I could get away.'

Mrs Lee's love life was never simple and straightforward. While she was engaged to her husband's friend, she was also writing to two young soldiers who were fighting in North Africa. One was named C.J.B. Oliver and the other, Alwyn Smith. In Oliver's case, the pen-friendship blossomed into romance and by the time she decided to move to Cape Town she considered herself engaged to Oliver.

Shortly before Mrs Lee left for Cape Town, she met Alwyn Smith at Polley's Hotel in Pretoria. He returned from North Africa as World War II drew to a close. Hostilities in North Africa had ceased many months earlier. On the train to Cape Town, he suddenly appeared in her carriage. 'I remember clearly saying to him "this is only for ladies,"' she would later claim.

The next morning, they had breakfast together and from then on they had all their meals together on the train. When they arrived in Cape Town, Smith took her to La Bella Alliance, a boarding house in the Gardens. That afternoon, they went for a drink at the Carlton Hotel. Mrs Lee was flattered by all the attention she was receiving.

'After that we became good friends,' she said. 'He immediately took so much interest in me that I was surprised. He told me that he had fallen in love with me.'

Smith, who had to return to Pretoria temporarily to obtain his discharge from the army, wanted them to marry before he left. Mrs Lee, however, was in two minds, although the idea was an attractive one.

'He said he was a major and I had a few pennies. I decided it might be good for me to get married to him. In any case he was a healthy man.'

But, the next day she had changed her mind.

'How could I break off my engagement to a man [Oliver] who was fighting for his country up North?'

A few days later, they went to a party in Bellville where Mrs Lee found out that Smith had told all his friends that they were going to get married. Rather than make a fool of him in public she played along. 'I was always a game,' she would say. That night, after they had been to Suikerbossie for further celebrations, they spent the night together. By the time Smith left for Pretoria, they were officially engaged.

Smith was away for six weeks and when he returned, Mrs Lee had moved to 6 Prince Street, Oranjezicht. He wanted them to marry the day after his return, but she was still a little uncertain. 'I said we could get married later,' she said, 'but he was very disappointed. He said that if I gave him a motorcar as a present he would know he meant something to me. I replied light-heartedly that I would give him a car if he wanted one. I knew you could not get cars at that time and thought that by the time they were available he would have forgotten about it.'

Photograph courtesy of Anne Fischer

Maria Lee

Then Smith started borrowing money from her – £150 the first time and then £500 later on.

'We were very much in love and I would do anything for him,' she explained.

Smith promised to repay the money by giving her some building society shares that he owned. She signed the paper that he produced and soon after he paid a cheque for £501 10d into her account. All this time, he kept pestering her to marry him, but she continued to refuse – officially she was still engaged to Mr Oliver.

In February 1946, Smith told her he was in trouble with an old girlfriend who was now married and asked Mrs Lee to give him £500 which he claimed he needed to sort the situation out. To add to all the confusion, in the same month she travelled to Pretoria to marry Oliver. This was to be her fourth and final marriage.

The Olivers set up home in Bethlehem, but all the time she was living with Oliver she was also keeping in secret contact with Smith. Smith was desperate for her to return to him so that they could get married. Not surprisingly, within months her marriage was on the rocks. She left her new husband and returned to Cape Town, where she worked for the American Swiss Watch Company. As the marriage lasted only a few months, she reverted to the name of Mrs Lee. By this time, she had decided that Smith was the only one for her.

Despite this, she refused to live with Smith until her divorce came through and, to solve the problem, Smith moved to Durban for a time and obtained work as a travelling salesman.

Alwyn Smith returned to Cape Town in October 1946. Shortly after his return, he telephoned Maria at work to inform her that he had received a telegram conveying the message that her mother had died. She became so distressed that her employers sent her home.

At first Smith was very sympathetic, but then he began drinking and became abusive. He wanted her to stop crying. 'A person who is dead is dead' he said. Then he flashed a thick wad of notes under her nose.

'I'm going to Durban to swank it,' he said.

'I was very annoyed with him about it,' said Mrs Lee, 'and chastised him for saying such a thing.'

While working for American Swiss, she was accused of stealing jewellery worth several thousand pounds. When her thefts were finally discovered, she was dismissed.

To make matters worse, she thought the money he had shown her was the £1 000 she had recently given him. Nevertheless, she trusted Smith enough to ask him to go to her deceased mother's farm in the Lichtenberg district, in the Transvaal, and wind up her estate. It was around this time that he started to get sick. He began complaining about stomach pains in December 1946.

By the beginning of 1947, the relationship between Mrs Lee and Smith was showing signs of strain, which is not surprising since she had been adding ant poison containing arsenic to his food for about two months.

Smith was drinking heavily and had also taken to gambling. Abdul Raman, a general dealer from Woodstock, testified at the trial how Smith regularly borrowed money from him for this purpose. He would borrow £20 or £25 in the morning and return it later the same day. On one occasion, Smith couldn't repay the money on time because he had a bad run at poker. He said he'd get the money from his wife and return it the next day. Raman also said that Smith was often drunk.

In February 1947, Miss Jane Jacobs, the daughter of Mrs Lee's landlady, heard the two of them arguing. The argument concerned the ownership of a car which Mrs Lee had paid for.

'Why should you get everything?' she demanded. 'Why can't I have the car in my own name?'

But Smith wasn't put off by her. 'Remember, I know a lot about you,' he threatened.

Perhaps this was a threat to blackmail her over the jewellery business as she had never been formally charged? – but we will never know. In court, she denied that she had ever stolen anything. Whatever the reason, by this time Smith had shown himself to be lazy, unambitious, and a drunkard. He was beginning to make Mrs Lee's life a misery. Getting rid of Smith would not only solve a lot of Maria's problems, it would also benefit her financially as he had a life insurance policy for £3 000 naming her as the sole benefactor.

In the autumn of 1947, Smith's condition deteriorated. On 13 March, 1947, Dr Morris Helman was summoned to Prince Street by Mrs Lee as Smith was complaining of abdominal pains and vomiting. Dr Helman prescribed a tonic and for a few days Smith showed signs of improvement. On 20 March, however, Dr Helman was called out for a second time. This time Smith was in a more serious condition. He had a rash on his body, was retching continuously, and complaining of acute stomach pains. On 22 March, he was admitted to hospital with suspected scarlet fever. However, the tests proved negative. Nevertheless, Smith's condition quickly improved while he was in hospital and he was discharged a week later.

Not long afterwards, Smith became seriously ill once more and Dr Helman was again called. By this time, he had come to suspect that Smith's system had been poisoned in some way. His patient, however, had lost all faith in the medical profession, preferring to treat himself, and dismissed Dr Helman.

For a month he had no contact with his patient and professional etiquette prevented him from contacting Smith.

Eventually, on 2 May, he received a telephone call from a distraught Mrs Lee claiming that Smith was dying and wanted him to come over. When Dr Helman subsequently examined Smith, he immediately suspected arsenic poisoning, but to confirm his diagnosis he wished to consult with a specialist. With Mrs Lee's approval, he summoned Dr Phillip Leftwich.

Dr Leftwich arrived at the house late on the afternoon of 2 May. He privately confirmed his colleague's diagnosis and suggested that the patient be sent to hospital. Mrs Lee objected since this might 'kill' him, but within hours Alwyn Smith was dead.

Mrs Lee appeared devastated by her lover's death and when Constable Harold Norman Bishop and Constable van Rooyen arrived in the mortuary van to take Smith's body away for post-mortem examination, she pulled the covering blanket away from Smith's ankles in order to kiss his feet.

The following day, Dr E.N. Keen of the Anatomy School at the University of Cape Town conducted a post-mortem. It was found that Smith's liver contained 0,41 grains of arsenic, the kidneys, 0,05 grains, and the fluid of the kidneys and stomach, 0,55 grains. His hair also contained traces of arsenic. It was likely, according to Dr Hillel Shapiro, the government pathologist, that the dose which finally killed Smith had been administered some time during the 24-hour period prior to death.

Despite an overwhelming body of evidence which proved that Smith had been poisoned, there was no direct evidence linking Mrs Lee to the crime and no arsenic was ever found in her possession. Consequently, for some months a police team, under the leadership of Detective Head Constable F. van Niekerk, investigated Smith's death and Maria Lee's life, associates and affairs.

During the months that followed, Mrs Lee was convinced that she had escaped the law, and in September 1947, she decided to leave Cape Town and move back to Pretoria.

On 14 October, she was arrested in Pretoria on suspicion of having murdered Alwyn Smith. She was remanded in custody at the Pretoria Central Prison while arrangements were made for her transfer back to Cape Town for the preliminary hearing.

It was while she was in prison that Mrs Lee finally sealed her fate.

Sharing a cell with Mrs Lee was one Margrieta Minaar. It seemed that Mrs Lee had already decided that her defence would be that Smith committed suicide by taking arsenic. But, she decided that she needed an accomplice to substantiate the story. Mrs Lee asked Minaar to say Smith had lived in Durban and had also been ill there. 'I was to say that he always complained of pains in the stomach; that he drank heavily and carried a powder which he took whenever he had a few drinks,' Minaar later told the court.

As an inducement, Mrs Lee offered to pay Mrs Minaar's bail money of £50 and give her a further £100 in 'expenses' if she would go to Cape Town and meet with two of Mrs Lee's friends – Mrs Peggy Smith and Mr Tommy Arpin. Mrs Minaar was also to tell Mr Kraai, a salesman friend of Mrs Lee's – the man who would pay the bail money – that she (Minaar) had known Smith in Durban in 1942, and that he had confessed to her that he intended to commit suicide using arsenic.

Mrs Minaar did as she promised. She spoke to Mr Kraai, who passed on the information to Mrs Lee's attorneys. However, Mrs Minaar also made a statement to the police on 20 October, the day she was released, and it was this statement which was to be the final nail in Mrs Lee's coffin.

Mrs Lee's trial eventually opened on 6 April, 1948. The case attracted widespread public interest and the public gallery was packed for every day of the five-week trial. Mrs Lee dressed-up for the occasion and became something of a celebrity.

The prosecution set out to prove three things. Firstly, that arsenic was the cause of Smith's death; secondly, that Mrs Lee was the only person who could have administered the arsenic; and thirdly, that these claims were supported by Mrs Minaar's evidence.

The most damning evidence of all was the fact that Mrs Minaar was aware that Smith had died of arsenic poisoning on 20 October, long before this fact had been reported in any of the newspapers. She also knew that the doctors were baffled by Smith's ailments. These two pieces of information could only have been obtained from one source: Mrs Lee. In turn, Mrs Lee could only have known that arsenic was the poison used if she had administered it herself.

Although Mrs Lee's defence attorney tried to undermine Mrs Minaar's credibility, he could not shake her evidence.

Mr Justice Steyn gave his judgement on 10 May, 1948. He found Mrs Lee guilty of murder.

'Do you wish to say anything before I pass sentence of death on you?' he asked.

'I repeat, I am not guilty,' she replied.

Mrs Lee lodged an appeal which was eventually dismissed on 11 September, 1948.

On the morning of Saturday, 18 September, 1948, Mrs Lee was hanged at the Pretoria Central Prison.

8.

THE THEFT OF THE OPPENHEIMER JEWELS

(1955)

On the night of 5 December, 1955, an assortment of jewels belonging to Bridget Oppenheimer, Harry Oppenheimer's wife, was stolen from *Little Brenthurst*. Their house lay in the grounds of *Brenthurst*, Ernest Oppenheimer's palatial mansion in Parktown, Johannesburg.

The most valuable item taken was a pure-white diamond ring estimated to be worth £35 000. A number of other exquisite pieces, valued at anything from £20 000 each, were also stolen. The total collection, valued at over £200 000, was insured for £250 000. (In current terms, that translates to around R5-million.)

It transpired that, sometime between 7.15 and 10.30 p.m. on the night in question, the thief or thieves walked into the grounds of *Brenthurst*, made their way up to Mrs Oppenheimer's bedroom in *Little Brenthurst*, removed the jewels, which were kept in a safe concealed in a built-in cupboard, and then walked out again. They needed neither sophisticated cutting tools nor explosives to get at the valuables, since they were able to use the safe key which Mrs Oppenheimer had left – as was her habit – in a little box which she kept conveniently nearby. They carried the jewels away in a small pillowcase.

None of the domestic servants heard or saw any of this. When Mrs Oppenheimer returned from her dinner engagement that evening, she didn't bother to return the jewellery she had been wearing to the safe. Although she did notice that a pillowslip was missing from the room, she didn't attach any particular significance to the fact. It wasn't until she opened the safe the following morning that she realised she had been robbed. She first telephoned the police, then her husband's office (Mr Oppenheimer was on a safari in Central Africa at the time); then she summoned the servants.

'I told them what had happened,' she said, 'that my jewels had apparently been stolen. But they knew nothing about the robbery.'

Police-Colonel Ulf Boberg, Divisional Criminal Investigation Officer for the Witwatersrand, took charge of the investigation, and within a short time a large team of police officers was on the scene. An exhaustive search of the grounds proved fruitless. Given the ease with which the crime had been carried out, it was suspected that the robbery had been an 'inside job' involving one or more members of the domestic staff. However, it quickly became apparent that this was not the case.

Photographs of the jewels were despatched to Interpol, Scotland Yard and the FBI, and police and customs throughout the country were ordered to be on the lookout. Carried by newspapers and radio services, news of the theft quickly spread worldwide.

On 9 December, a reward of £20 000 was offered for information leading to the return of the jewels.

The valuables were insured by the London & Lancashire Company, in London. One week after the robbery, a firm of adjusters which represented the insurers sent their own chief investigator, Mr Dudley Strevens, to South Africa.

On his arrival in Johannesburg, Mr Strevens immediately contacted the firm of John Murray & Company, the South African representatives of the London insurers, and on 13 December, he met with one of their insurance assessors, Mr A.D. Cook. It emerged that the latter gentleman had been approached by an Australian named William Lindsay Pearson, who claimed to have information regarding the missing jewels: he maintained he knew not only who had them, but also where they were, and he was prepared to arrange their return – in exchange for a reward considerably higher than the £20 000 offered. Mr Cook had not yet informed the police of Pearson's approach.

Shortly after Strevens' arrival, the two insurance men went to meet Pearson at his room in the Old Carlton Hotel in Eloff Street. The Australian stated his case in no uncertain terms.

'Gentlemen,' he began, 'I've been a swindler and confidence trickster all my life, and I've no intention of changing now. I've got information, but you're not going to get it out of me for the reward offered. You're going to have to pay a lot more before those jewels are back in Mrs Oppenheimer's safe.' Pearson was undoubtedly a cool customer, but Dudley Strevens was no fool either.

'Mr Pearson,' he replied sharply, 'My company is not in the jewellery business. We have no intention of buying back the jewels. We are looking for information that will lead to their recovery.'

Pearson nodded. 'Yes, I quite understand. Unfortunately, the thieves will not consider returning them for less than £75 000' – Strevens resolutely shook his head – 'but I may be able to persuade them to drop this figure to £50 000.'

'That amount is out of the question,' Strevens replied. 'In England, the reward paid is normally 10% of the value of the stolen articles, which in this case means £20 000. We might raise this figure to £40 000, but I stress the key word is "might". Furthermore, any negotiations with the robbers would have to be conducted through official police channels.'

At the mention of the word 'police', Pearson took fright. One of his concerns was that if the police became involved, they would investigate his shady background and deport him. It was at this point that he came up with a second scheme.

He proposed that if Strevens or Cook obtained a gun licence on his behalf, he would hijack the jewels himself. The two insurance men were totally against this idea and pointed out that, besides, it was impossible to get a gun licence. Pearson then presented a third scheme, a compromise of sorts. He would accept the figure of £20 000 on the understanding that he would, in addition, be paid a further £20 000 'retainer' by Strevens' firm, in the form of four annual instalments of £5 000 each, for which he would not have to perform any work. Again Strevens refused. After a long process of negotiation, Pearson reluctantly agreed to accept a reward of £20 000.

With a deal of sorts finally worked out, Pearson now told his story. He maintained that a month or so earlier, while having a drink at the Victoria Hotel, he had met a man named Percival William Radley. At the time, Radley, who it would later turn out was a convicted felon who had spent over 10 years in British prisons for a variety of crimes, had hinted that a 'big job' involving jewels was about to be carried out.

Between 23 November and 8 December, Pearson had been in London, but, reading of the theft of the Oppenheimer jewels on his return to South Africa, he immediately realised that this was the 'big job' to which Radley had referred. His suspicions were confirmed when he contacted Radley, and it was then that he decided to make himself some easy money.

On 14 December, the day after Strevens and Cook had met with Pearson, Colonel Boberg learnt of the discussion. He was extremely angry at having been excluded, and soon the three men were on their way to meet with Pearson at the Carlton Hotel.

When Boberg confronted Pearson, the Australian was very cool about the whole affair. Boberg challenged him to produce any item of jewellery to prove his story. Naturally, Pearson could not oblige. However, he did agree to act as go-between in a scheme to get the jewels back. He already had his part carefully worked out: he would claim to be acting on behalf of an internationally famous crime boss named 'Lucky' Luciano. He would summon his 'contact man' – Radley – to his hotel suite, where a member of Luciano's gang – a disguised policeman – would be waiting with the money.

A meeting with Radley was duly arranged for that same evening. A large contingent of plain-clothes policemen descended on the hotel and Detective-Sergeant Swart, the man who was to play the role of Lucky Luciano's henchman, hid in Pearson's bathroom. He had with him two suitcases containing £48 000 in cancelled notes.

At about 9.15 p.m., Pearson received a telephone call in his room. Fifteen minutes later, two men knocked at the door. One was Percival Radley and the other a 34-year-old former security officer named Donald Miles. Miles was carrying a box wrapped in Christmas paper. Pearson carried the box into the bathroom, where Detective-Sergeant Swart was hiding. Shortly afterwards, Swart said, 'You can tell your men I'm satisfied. I'll buy the jewels.' And he handed over the money.

While Radley and Miles were counting the money on the bed, Swart slipped into the corridor and summoned his waiting colleagues. Within seconds, Radley and Miles had been arrested for the theft of the Oppenheimer jewels. The two men were taken to Marshall Square Police Station for questioning.

It was at this point that things began to go wrong for the police. Both Radley and Miles denied vehemently that they had had anything to do with the robbery. Radley claimed that he had been invited to Pearson's room for a social drink and Miles declared ignorance of the whole affair. He maintained that he had been given the Christmas parcel by a 'Jewish chap' and asked to deliver it to suite 641 – Pearson's suite. 'I've been taken for a ride,' he said.

To make matters worse, Pearson suddenly developed cold feet over the whole affair; whether he was suffering pangs of conscience or was concerned about his reputation among the criminal fraternity is impossible to say. Without his testimony, however, the police had no case.

Help came from an unexpected source. On the day following his arrest, Percival Radley declared that he was prepared to co-operate with the police if he was guaranteed immunity from prosecution. The police agreed to this condition.

In his statement, Radley admitted that he had originally been prepared for involvement in the robbery. He also confessed to entering the grounds of *Brenthurst* with Miles and 'casing' the house. However, on the night in question he had been at the cinema with a girlfriend. It was Miles alone, he claimed, who had broken into *Little Brenthurst* and stolen the Oppenheimer jewels.

A preparatory examination was held at Johannesburg Magistrates' Court in January 1956. Miles was charged with theft and housebreaking with intent to steal. Pearson, whom the Crown alleged was in no way involved in the actual theft, was to be charged with accessory before and after the fact. Radley, a colourful character who gave the public vivid glimpses of the underworld, was the prosecution's chief witness.

On 16 March, the Attorney-General announced that he would not prosecute Pearson. Miles, however, was committed to trial on the charge that, on the night of 5 December, 1955, he had stolen from the home of Harry and Bridget Oppenheimer: 16 rings, nine bracelets, 17 brooches, five necklaces, six watches, an evening bag, two buddhas set in platinum with diamonds, a powder case, a festoon ornament, a platinum-and-diamond bag, two tiepins, a buddha without stones, 50 to 60 Rhodesian bank notes, a wallet containing notes, safe keys, three jewellery boxes, a number of badges and cigarette holders, and a pillow slip.

Miles' trial before a nine-man jury began at the Witwatersrand Criminal Sessions on 3 April, 1956. Pearson attended the trial, but was called by neither party. The prosecution alleged that Miles, who had worked at *Little Brenthurst* for a roofing contractor in 1954, had knowledge of the jewels. The evidence against him was based, in the main, on the testimony of Radley, a person the prosecution admitted was a confirmed criminal and of dubious character. He was also an accomplice to the crime.

Miles' defence was that he had been duped by Radley and had no knowledge of the theft. The first time he had discussed it was a few days after the theft had been reported in the newspapers. When he was asked how the jewels came to be in his possession, he claimed that he was employed by Radley and was to be paid £250 for carrying a cardboard box wrapped in Christmas paper up to the hotel room. (Notice that this contradicts his original statement when he was arrested.) He did not know what was in the box, but was under the impression that it contained a number of uncut diamonds which were being sold by a syndicate to an unlicensed buyer. It was only after he had been arrested in Pearson's room that he realized he had been carrying the Oppenheimer jewels. He alleged that Radley had stolen them.

The trial was over after six days. Although Miles had been questioned closely, the prosecution had failed to shake his story.

On 9 April, the judge gave his summing-up of the case: it took only 25 minutes. In less than an hour the jury had returned with a verdict of not guilty.

So, no-one was punished for the theft of the Oppenheimer jewels. Pearson received a reward of £20 000 from the London & Lancashire Company, of which he was obliged to pay £6 000 to the South African Receiver of Revenue. He was subsequently asked to leave the country, as was Radley.

Perhaps the best summary of the whole affair appeared in the *Cape Times* shortly after the trial had closed:

> *We now know of three men who did not steal the jewels. But this does not help us to know who did. Perhaps we never shall and the whole affair, except for a small dent in the profits of an insurance company, will be forgotten.*

9.

THE ABORTION SCANDAL

(DR GERHARDUS BUCHNER: 1949)

Just before midnight on Wednesday, 9 November, 1948, the police raided the private medical practice of Dr Gerhardus Bernieres Buchner at Castle Mansions, Eloff Street, Johannesburg. They discovered five women in different rooms, each of whom had undergone an abortion.

Buchner was in another room, counting money on the bed.

When Detective Head Constable F.C. van Niekerk, the officer in charge of the raid, accused Buchner of carrying out abortions on the premises, Buchner claimed that the women were being treated for varicose veins. One of the patients was immediately transferred to the Johannesburg General Hospital where it was established that she had received an abortion. Thus began one of South Africa's greatest scandals in recent times.

Buchner (44) was an outstanding physician. He studied medicine at the University of Cape Town Medical School, in Germany and at the Sorbonne in Paris. He had been operating an extremely lucrative abortion clinic in Johannesburg for over eight years and his private practice at Castle Mansions provided the perfect front for these clandestine operations.

The system at Castle Mansions was simple, effecient and well-organised. On arrival, patients would be examined either by Dr Buchner or his junior partner, Dr Edward Blumberg (34). Once pregnancy had been confirmed, Nurse Sussanna Pieterse (34), would present the bill. (The average cost was £70 to £75, payable in advance.) When the financial details were concluded, arrangements for the abortion would be made. Normally, patients would arrive sometime during the afternoon, go into the theatre late in the evening, and be discharged the following morning.

They would not know the names of the doctors or the nurses that treated them.

The abortion team comprised four people. Buchner or Blumberg carried out the operation with Nurse Pieterse acting as anaesthetist. A second nurse, Anna Sophia Kelly, sometimes performed the duties of general assistant. In addition, a relief nurse who filled in for Kelly in 1941, when she went on holiday, provided a referral system. From 1943 to 1945, this nurse had worked for another doctor, but would send pregnant women to Buchner. For this service, she received a commission of £5 to £7 per patient. In 1946, she worked in the Castle Mansion rooms once more and was paid £30 per month – an excellent salary at the time.

At the inquiry that followed Buchner's exposure, the same nurse claimed that at least five abortions were carried out each day – although the clinic had on occasion handled up to nine patients in a twenty-four hour period. In some cases, operations were conducted by torch-light in order to avoid attracting unnecessary attention to the premises!

Despite the elaborate precautions which Buchner and his associates took to maintain their anonymity, word slowly got around. In the end, exposure was inevitable. Buchner had a close shave in 1946, when the Johannesburg newspaper, *Weekblad*, published an article entitled *Aborsie in Johannesburg*, in which it was alleged that one of Johannesburg's foremost abortionists had three flats in the city, all under different names and was said to be making £2 500 a month from the practice.

The newspaper's source was subsequently proved to be more than accurate. Indeed, exactly how lucrative Buchner's practice had become was revealed during the trial. Financial records presented to the court showed that from July 1946 to June 1947, over £51 000 had been paid into Buchner's banking account. From August 1947, to July 1948, the figure was £36 000, and in the three months that preceded the police raid, Buchner's income had been £9 500! Buchner also owned a farm and plots of ground on which houses were built and sold. The abortion clinic at the Castle Mansions was making him very wealthy.

The end came for Buchner shortly after the police were informed about the illegal operations being performed at Castle Mansions by a small stock farmer from the Northern Transvaal.

The farmer had been asked by his recently-widowed cousin to take her to Johannesburg where she was to have a medical examination for 'varicose veins'. After the first visit to Castle Mansions, she had asked him to lend her £75, for the cost of the operation. She had no money of her own because her husband's estate had not been wound-up. Her uncle gave her £70, and a few days later they returned to the city. When he picked her up after her operation, she looked 'very weak and pale' and on the return journey, she confessed to having had an abortion. The farmer later returned to Castle Mansions, spoke first to Nurse Pieterse and then to Buchner and tried unsuccessfully to get some of their money back. It was not long afterwards that he approached Brigadier Mickdal, Acting Commissioner for the police in Pretoria, and alleged that Buchner was 'procuring illegal abortions on a wholesale scale'.

Following the raid on Castle Mansions, the police began an intensive investigation to trace other patients of Buchner and Blumberg. Needless to say, the investigation was of an extremely sensitive nature, all the more so since the police had no wish to cause hardship or distress to any of the women who had been treated by either of the two doctors.

Meanwhile, Buchner, Blumberg and Pieterse were remanded in custody pending an inquiry. The inquiry which began on 9 December, 1948, quickly established that there was a case to answer. The four accused were granted bail, Buchner and Blumberg for the amounts of £500 each.

On 17 January, 1949, the official hearing began at the Johannesburg Magistrates' Court under Mr M.A.S. Mathews. In order to protect the identities of those involved, the hearing was held in-camera and none of the names and addresses of the over sixty witnesses who were called to give evidence were released to the press. At the end of each day an official bulletin was issued.

Buchner, Blumberg, Pieterse and Kelly were subsequently committed for trial on 1 March, 1949.

The seven-week trial which began two months later was to attract immense public interest, produce over 1 100 pages of written evidence, and reveal some astounding facts. The prosecution was led by Mr F.E. Lutge K.C., Attorney-General for the Transvaal.

Witness after witness came to the stand and testified that they had had abortions performed by Buchner and Blumberg under conditions of great secrecy. In virtually every case the patient had no knowledge of the names of the doctors or nurses who treated them.

One woman told the court how, on the morning after the operation, she was brought a cup of tea in her room and noticed that there were a number of other cups on the tray. She had assumed that this meant that other patients were also being treated. She also said that on the day after her operation she was sent home in a taxi, even though she was still very weak, because her room had to be vacated by noon.

One woman from Natal went to Johannesburg to procure an abortion after doctors in Natal refused to help her. She approached a number of doctors and all but one refused to help her in any way – he gave her Buchner's name.

At Castle Mansions, she was first interviewed by a blond nurse (Pieterse) and was later examined by a doctor who told her that she was five months pregnant. The blond woman then asked her if she couldn't get married. Pieterse then informed her that, because of the advanced state of her pregnancy, the fee for the operation would be £200. This figure was later reduced to £150. The woman paid £90 in cash – all the money she had with her – and Pieterse also took down her parents' names and address.

'Why did Nurse Pieterse do that?' Mr N. Masters, Mr Lutge's assistant asked.

'As a guarantee,' the woman replied.

'Guarantee? Guarantee of what?'

'That they would tell my parents if I didn't pay the money I owed.'

She later sent the balance by post.

Dr Blumberg was also charged with attempting to defeat the ends of justice. He was alleged to have approached a policeman friend (who happened by coincidence to have been part of the raid on Castle Mansions) and asked him to get the names and addresses of some of the key witnesses. The police initially maintained that this was an attempt by Blumberg to get some of the witnesses to either change their evidence or claim that their evidence was given under duress. These charges were later dropped.

After hearing evidence for seven weeks the judges retired on 27 June to consider their verdict.

At 10 a.m. on the morning of Tuesday, 9 August, 1949, judgment was finally given.

Facing a packed courtroom, the judge began his two-hour summing-up. He began by commending the detective team of Detective Head Constable F.C. van Niekerk, Detective Head Constable H.P. Mare and Detective-Sergeants J.A. le Roux and S. Smidt. They had carried out extremely delicate investigative work with great tact and consideration. Consequently, neither the lives nor the reputations of any of the women involved had been harmed in any way.

The judge turned to the defendants. The court had accepted, he conceded, the defence counsel's argument that the women who had appeared for the prosecution were in no way complainants. All those called had appeared merely at the request of the police. However, as he pointed out, the morality of abortion was not the issue. It was the task of the court simply to establish if the law had been broken and this was clearly the case. Furthermore, the accused were fully aware of the illegality of what they were doing: they had operated under conditions of great secrecy, and the names and addresses of the women who had undergone abortions did not appear on any file cards. It was clear, therefore, that Buchner's private practice at Castle Mansions was being used to procure abortions on a regular basis.

Of the 60 counts on which Buchner was charged, he was found guilty of 49. he was given six weeks 'hard labour' for each count – a total of five years and 34 weeks. Blumberg was given six weeks 'hard labour' for 34 counts – three years and 48 weeks. Nurse Pieterse, who had actively participated in the abortions and acted as anaesthetist, was given four weeks on each of 48 counts – a total of four years. Nurse Kelly received four weeks for ten counts but her four months sentence was suspended. Buchner, Blumberg and Kelly received their sentences stoically and made no protest as they were led away to the cells. Pieterse, however, broke down completely and had to be assisted from the court.

And so it seemed that a long and drawn out *cause célèbre* had finally ended. But the closing chapter of the story was still to be written. Buchner was to use his medical knowledge to save a life while in prison. For this 'exemplary conduct' he was granted two years remission of sentence.

Dr Gerhardus Buchner died several years after his release.

10.

THE MYSTIFYING DEATH OF 'BUBBLES' SCHROEDER

(1949)

Within days of her murder, everyone had heard of 'Bubbles' Schroeder. But why did her death attract such unprecedented public interest? For one thing, she was young and desirable. She was also what was euphemistically called a 'good-time girl'. And, of course, she was dead. But was there something else? Something less tangible? Perhaps it was that, to many people, she typified the new, post-war age: a world of fast cars, fast living and easy virtue.

Jacoba 'Bubbles' Schroeder was born in Lichtenburg on 8 June, 1931. She was educated at Benoni and Vereeniging. When she was four years old, her mother had to go out to work, and she was cared for by a cousin in Vereeniging until she was 13. For the next four years she lived with her mother in Johannesburg. Then, in March 1948, she returned to Vereeniging to work for a coal agency but, unbeknown to her relatives, she moved back to Johannesburg two months later. Soon after her return to the city, she moved into the apartment of a fifty-two-year-old bookmaker named Philip Stein, whom she had met at a dance in Orange Grove. Although Stein liked having Bubbles around, he soon realized that his new guest could sometimes be a lot more trouble than he had bargained for. Bubbles was in the habit of throwing a tantrum when she couldn't get her own way.

'She was a young woman, a little loose in her morals,' Stein said. 'But she was very sweet – except when she was drunk. Then she became unmanageable.'

Matters finally came to a head early in June 1949. Bubbles had come home drunk once too often and Stein asked her to leave. Shortly after this, she moved to Dorchester Mansions in Rissik Street, where she shared an apartment with a girlfriend named Mrs Griffin, who was a 'hostess'.

Although Bubbles never held down a regular job in all the time she was living in Johannesburg, she was never short of money. Nor was there a dearth of men willing to pay for the pleasure of her company.

'Bubbles was a glamour girl,' Mrs Griffin would say. 'She'd spend her days at the beauty parlour and her nights at night clubs. And she could be most charming. Until she had a few drinks in her, of course. Then she became obstinate and difficult.'

On Thursday, 11 August, 1949, Morris Bilchik visited Dorchester Mansions. He made a date with Bubbles for the following Saturday night, and the two duly went out together. At the end of the evening, they went back to Bilchik's home and spent the night together.

On the following Monday morning, Bilchik boasted of his conquest to his friend, David Polliack (21). At lunchtime, the two men visited Bubbles at her apartment. The plan was that she would get hold of her girlfriend, Penny, and the four of them could go out together that night. Unfortunately, Penny was nowhere to be found. In the end, they decided simply to make up a threesome.

After Bilchik and Polliack had left, Bubbles went to visit Phillip Stein. She spent the afternoon at his apartment, where she had a few glasses of brandy, and then returned home at 6 p.m.. When she reached Dorchester Mansions, Bilchik and Polliack were already waiting for her. She apologized for keeping them waiting and invited them inside while she changed into a green dress and put on some make-up. Around 7.30 p.m. they set out for Polliack's house, *Hlatikulu*, in the plush suburb of Illovo. (Polliack's mother was in Durban at the time, so the three of them had the house virtually to themselves.) Bubbles travelled with David Polliack, while Bilchik took his own car.

They reached the house at about eight o'clock, just as Polliack's cousin, Hyman Balfour Liebman (20), was leaving for Houghton to pick up his girlfriend. Polliack and Bilchik invited Liebman to bring his girlfriend back to the house to join the party, but Liebman declined. They had already arranged to go to the cinema for the evening.

After Liebman had driven off, the other three went into the house. Polliack asked Irene, the cook, to prepare some food, and at about 9.30 p.m. they sat down to eat a meal of tinned asparagus soup, followed by chops with chips. For dessert they had a can of tinned peaches. Afterwards, they went into the living-room. Bubbles drank a few glasses of brandy and snacked from a tin of peanuts.

At about 11.15 p.m. Bilchik left for home. It seemed obvious to him that Bubbles and Polliack wanted to be left alone.

After Bilchik had left, Bubbles and Polliack cleared up in the living-room, then went upstairs to listen to records in Polliack's bedroom. Not long afterwards, Bilchik phoned. Jealousy, it seemed, had finally got the better of him. First he spoke to Bubbles, then he apologized to Polliack for disturbing them. After about fifteen minutes, he rang off.

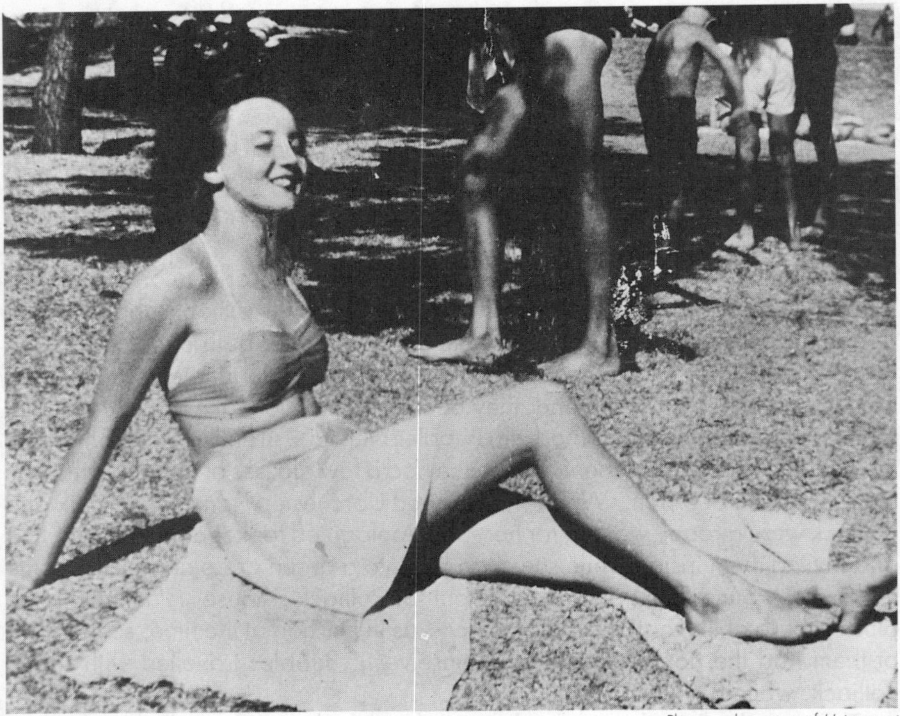

Photograph courtesy of *Huisgenoot*

Bubbles Schroeder

Around midnight Hyman Liebman returned from his cinema date. (Although he lived in the Brits district, he often stayed at *Hlatikulu* when Mrs Polliack was away.) Polliack met him in the hallway and told him that Bubbles was in his room. The trouble was that she'd had too much to drink and he wanted to get her home before she passed out.

Liebman went upstairs to see for himself. It was clear to him, he later said, that Bubbles had been drinking, but she was far from drunk. She insisted on having another drink. Eventually, Liebman got her a glass of weak brandy.

At about 12.30 a.m., Bubbles suddenly wanted to go home. Her mother was staying with her, she said, and expected her back by 1.00 a.m. Eventually, at about 1.30 a.m., the three of them walked out onto the driveway, where the cars were parked. Polliack wanted to take her home, but she got into Liebman's car and wouldn't get out.

In the end, Liebman offered to drive her home and, with Bubbles complaining that she wanted to drive, they set out for Dorchester Mansions. Fifteen to twenty minutes later, Liebman pulled back into the driveway. This time, he was alone.

'That girl's a lunatic,' he told his friend. 'She wanted to drive and when I wouldn't let her she made me stop and got out. I told her to be sensible but she wouldn't listen.'

Polliack was angry.

'You mean you let her walk? Where did you let her out?' he asked.

'At the Dunkeld bus terminus.'

'And did she say anything?'

Liebman nodded. 'Yes. She said, "Which way to town?" I told her to follow the bus wires along Oxford Road. The last thing she said to me was, "You will be surprised to read about my corpse in the morning papers."'

'Don't you realize what can happen to the girl?' shouted Polliak.

'Yes, of course I do,' his friend snapped, 'but at this time of night I didn't think she'd come to any harm.'

Liebman was tired and fed up. 'I'm going to bed,' he added, and went into the house.

Polliack was worried about Bubbles. Although it was nearly 2.00 a.m., he set off in his own car to try to find her. About an hour later, he returned home. Bubbles Schroeder had vanished.

The two young men assumed that Bubbles had managed to get a lift with a passing motorist. Neither of them dreamt anything was wrong until Morris Bilchik phoned Polliack at work the next day. That morning, Bilchik had called at Dorchester Mansions to see Bubbles, but had learnt from her mother that she hadn't returned home from her night out. Soon after he had heard this news, Polliack went to see Mrs Schroeder himself. Later Bilchik, Polliack and Mrs Schroeder drove down to Rosebank Police Station to report that Bubbles was missing. Polliack also telephoned the general hospital to see if she had been admitted there.

Bubbles Schroeder's body was discovered, thirty hours after her death, at Birdhaven plantation by Samuel Ngibisa Mabela. The plantation was less than a kilometre from the spot where Liebman claimed to have dropped her off.

She was lying on her back among burnt-out grass about 30 metres from the road. Her face was turned to the right, and her left leg was laid over her right. Her left arm was pressed against the side of her body, while her right was flung out at an angle of about 75 degrees. She was hatless, shoeless, and her coat was missing. Although there were scratch marks and some bruising on her neck, there were no footprints around the body nor any signs of violent struggle.

The first thing that struck Dr J. Friedman, the Johannesburg District Surgeon, when he arrived at the scene of the crime, was the position of the body. From the way Bubbles was lying, it appeared that she had been placed carefully on the ground, which suggested that she had been murdered nearby and then carried (probably over the shoulder) into the plantation.

This assumption was substantiated by the fact that, although both of the victim's shoes were missing, there was neither grass nor soil on the soles of her feet. She certainly had not walked to the spot where her body was discovered.

The bodice of the green dress she wore was slightly ripped and one button was missing. The lower right leg of her stocking was also snagged in a number of places. Her panties were torn on the right side, but her black petticoat and black brassiere were intact. The post-mortem revealed that she had not been sexually assaulted.

In her mouth were some pieces of a hard, clay-like material. Although some of the bits lay deep in her throat, there were no particles in her lungs, proving that the clay had been forced into her mouth after death.

Dr Friedman examined the contents of Bubbles' stomach. The extent of digestion of the various foods particles he found was to entirely substantiate Polliack and Bilchik's subsequent account of events on the night of her death.

A highly significant fact that emerged during the post-mortem was that Miss Schroeder was suffering from a condition of the thymus gland which would have caused her to fall unconscious very quickly from only slight pressure around the neck. The bruising on her neck indicated that she had been strangled from behind, probably by a scarf or something similar, and had scratched herself in an effort to tear the ligature from her throat.

Mr Friedman concluded that the cause of death was asphyxia and inhibition due to pressure on her throat and the impaction of a hard, clay-like substance (similar to that in a heap of builder's lime a couple of metres away) in her hypopharynx. He estimated the time of death as around two o'clock on the morning of Tuesday, 16 August.

The police launched a large-scale search in the area around Birdhaven Plantation, but without success. However, on 13 October, almost two months after the murder, Hyman Liebman and David Polliack were arrested 'in connection with the murder of Bubbles Schroeder'. They appeared in court the following day and were remanded in custody. Later, they were granted bail of £5 000 and £500 respectively. Their trial began a few days later at the Johannesburg Magistrates' Court.

The evidence which the police presented to the court was almost entirely circumstantial. The prosecution based its case upon the fact that Liebman and Polliack had been with Miss Schroeder late on the night of her death. There was no direct evidence to suggest that either of the two men were connected in any way to her murder, however, and eventually they were acquitted.

So who did kill Bubbles Schroeder? The police contended that Liebman had strangled her in his car using a scarf. This was after he had driven her to Birdhaven Plantation and attempted to have sex with her. When she fell unconscious, he had carried her body away from the road. But there was not a shred of evidence – apart from the fact that Liebman did give her a lift in his car – to support this claim.

A second theory was that Bubbles was robbed and killed by a passing African. This hypothesis is supported by the fact that her mouth was stuffed with lime. (Among certain African peoples it is customary to place something in the mouth of a victim who has suffered a violent death, to prevent him or her from speaking ill of the killer in the afterworld.) But this theory has a number of obvious weaknesses. For example, if the motive for the crime was robbery, why was Bubbles killed? And why was the body so neatly laid out?

A third, and possibly the most plausible answer was advanced by the late Benjamin Bennett, who was crime writer for *The Argus* at the time. Bennett suggested that Bubbles probably tried to hitch a lift home and was picked up by a passing motorist. (If there had been two men in the car, the passenger would have moved into the back so that Bubbles could have the front seat.) She was assaulted – the man in the back was in a perfect position to put a scarf around her neck to restrain her – and 'accidentally' asphyxiated. Afterwards, her body was carried into the nearby plantation and dumped. Lime was put into her mouth simply to confuse the police into thinking the crime had been perpetrated by an African.

All this is mere conjecture, however, and we are still left with the question of who killed Bubbles Schroeder?. It seems unlikely that the truth will ever be known.

11.

THE WOMAN WHO TALKED HERSELF TO DEATH

(MARGARET RHEEDER: 1957)

If Margaret Elizabeth Rheeder had kept quiet after she had poisoned her husband to death with arsenic, she might well have got away with murder.

Margaret Rheeder (*nee* Harker) was born on 6 September, 1922, at Platbos, a tiny village just outside Knysna in the Cape. By the time her father died, she had six brothers and sisters. Later on, her mother married Cornelius Share, who fathered a further five children.

During her childhood, Margaret knew the meaning of abject poverty. The house was chronically overcrowded and the family sometimes went hungry. To make matters worse, her stepfather was a sickly man who was often out of work. At one time, they had to depend on an £8 monthly grant provided by the Department of Social Welfare.

In 1934, Cornelius Share died. Margaret and her sisters, Gwen and Olga, were sent to an orphanage in George, where they learnt domestic work. When Margaret was sixteen, she obtained her first job – working as a servant for a family in Paarl. About five years later, she moved briefly to Wynberg. At twenty-one, she returned to Knysna, where she took a job as a housekeeper in a local hotel.

It was in Knysna that she met and married her first husband. She had two children, but the marriage was not a happy one – her husband spent much time away from home and was always in trouble with the police. During his absences, she struck up friendships with other men, and she openly boasted of her 'conquests'. Ultimately, she divorced her husband while he was in prison.

In 1951, she met Benjamin Fredenman Rheeder on the platform at Great Brak station. It appeared that the couple had much in common: both had two children and were fleeing unhappy marriages. These similarities proved to be the basis of a warm friendship and it was not long before Margaret offered to keep house for him. He accepted her offer and she moved to Port Elizabeth with him. The relationship deepened and on 6 September, 1952 – Margaret's thirtieth birthday – the couple were married.

Ben Rheeder had a stable job as a checker at Port Elizabeth docks and, for the first time in her life, Margaret had a degree of financial security. For a while, the marriage seemed idyllic, on the surface at least. Then the arguments began. First she became critical of his children, then she began to complain about his drinking habits, and finally she accused him of flirting with other women. She made no effort to hide her dissatisfaction, and often complained to her sister, Gwen.

'I don't love him, Gwen,' she would say. 'I never did. He doesn't suit me. I only married him out of pity. I'd like to give him a...slow death...' Her next husband, she maintained, would be someone she 'really loved', not the 'old, licked-off bones' she was used to.

In October 1955, Margaret Rheeder's prayers were finally answered. She and her husband took in a lodger: a twenty-two-year-old railway worker named Johannes Strydom. The man's youth and vigour were exactly what Margaret was looking for. Not surprisingly, soon after he moved into the house, she took to visiting him in his bedroom while her husband was out at work. As time passed, she became more and more infatuated. On one occasion, she confided in Strydom that she desperately wanted to get rid of her husband.

'I once even smeared rat poison on his sandwiches, Johan,' she said, 'but Ben said they smelt funny and threw them away.'

'Then why don't you separate?' Strydom asked her. 'Why do you have to kill him?'

'Because I'd have to leave with nothing. And I couldn't bear to see him with another woman then,' she replied.

By the end of summer 1957, the Rheeder's marriage had degenerated into open hostility. To compound matters, Margaret was refusing to sleep with her husband because of his 'carryings-on'.

The final sequence of events which was to lead to the death of Benjamin Rheeder began on Saturday 27 April, 1957. That morning, Margaret went to a pharmacy in Kempston Road, Port Elizabeth, which was about three kilometres from her home, and purchased a bottle of *Antexit* ant-killer. She was served by the owner, Mr A. Redhouse, who warned her that the insecticide contained arsenic and was an extremely dangerous poison which had to be kept away from young children and pets. She thanked him for his advice and assured him that she would be most careful. Then she signed the poisons register and left.

The following Monday, Benjamin Rheeder became violently ill at work. He was still unwell the next day and visited the railway doctor, Dr Edmund Bloch, complaining of pains in the shoulder. The doctor diagnosed fibrositis and prescribed appropriate medication. That night, Rheeder took a turn for the worse. He began to retch almost uncontrollably and suffered excruciating pains in his legs. At around midnight, he took himself to the casualty department of the provincial hospital. Dr Bloch was summoned; he gave Benjamin an injection to alleviate the pain, and asked him to visit the surgery the following day.

On the Wednesday, Mrs Rheeder telephoned Dr Bloch and told him that her husband had greatly improved, but was not well enough to make his appointment. The doctor asked her to continue the medication he had prescribed and to keep him informed of the patient's progress. The next day, he visited Rheeder at his home. Although the patient complained of vague pains and general nausea, his condition did not appear to be serious. Dr Bloch fully expected him to be up and about in a few days.

Five days later, on 7 May, the doctor was called out again. By this time, Rheeder's condition had deteriorated considerably. His tongue was thick and white, he was suffering continual bouts of diarrhoea and vomiting, and was finding it difficult to breathe. Nevertheless, none of these symptoms appeared life-threatening. Dr Bloch suggested that the patient transfer to the local hospital for observation either that evening or the following morning, depending on when a bed was available. Failing this, he would arrange for a specialist to make a housecall to Rheeder.

Meanwhile, Margaret Rheeder seemed to assume that her husband's death was imminent. To one neighbour, Mrs Fourie, she talked about the insurance money she would receive when Ben passed away – hardly the sort of thought that should have concerned a loving wife at such a time. Other neighbours began to remark on the indifference she showed to her husband's suffering: on one occasion, she was seen to be calmly ironing in the kitchen while her husband cried out in pain in the bedroom.

That night, Kenneth Harker, Margaret's brother, who lived in the same street, went to visit his brother-in-law. Ben Rheeder was so seriously ill that he could hardly swallow. At about 10 p.m., Margaret spoon-fed her husband a darkish liquid, which Harker assumed was medicine, from a cup. Soon after this, Rheeder began to writhe in agony, clutching his stomach and moaning about the 'hellish fires' that consumed him. Margaret showed little sympathy. 'He's just putting it on,' she said.

In the early hours of 8 May, Benjamin Rheeder died. Dr Bloch was called and signed the death certificate. Cause of death was given as heart failure resulting from acute gastro-enteritis.

Despite the rapidly deteriorating condition of the corpse, Margaret refused to have her husband moved from the bedroom for two-and-a-half days. By having him buried straight from home, she expected to avoid the possibility of a post-mortem. She also made an attempt to deflect suspicion from herself through innuendo to the neighbours that the treatment her husband had received from Dr Bloch was anything but satisfactory. Dr Bloch, she claimed, had given her husband a 'deadly injection' and thereby hastened his end. He had 'put the knife' to Benjamin, she maintained, 'because he was trying to weed out all the Nationalists'. She repeated the accusation to her brother-in-law. But, when someone suggested that a post-mortem be held to substantiate these claims, she dismissed the idea.

'I don't need any proof,' she said. On another occasion, she claimed that Dr Bloch had turned to her after her husband had died and asked, 'What shall we write?' before completing the death certificate.

Before too long, people began to talk. Eventually, the rumours concerning the untimely death of Ben Rheeder reached the ears of one Detective-Constable Petrus Rheeder. Although he was unrelated to Benjamin, the fact that they shared a surname was enough to pique his interest. A number of low-key enquiries were made, then the Detective-Constable questioned Strydom. Shortly thereafter, an official investigation was instigated and, ten days after Benjamin Rheeder had been buried, the police called on Margaret Rheeder. They were particularly interested to know if there was any poison in the house. They took away for analysis a number of tablets, but all proved harmless.

The next step was to visit pharmacies in the locality. Within days, they came across Margaret Rheeder's name in the poisons register at Kempston Road Pharmacy. (For a time, the police kept this knowledge from her. When she was finally confronted with this evidence, she claimed she had bought the arsenic on her husband's instruction but that he had subsequently thrown it away as he had thought it too dangerous to have in the house.)

On 11 June, little over a month after the burial, Ben Rheeder's body was exhumed. Sections of his viscera (large internal organs) were sent to the Government Chemical Laboratories in Johannesburg for analysis. Traces of arsenic were found in the liver, the kidneys, the hair and nails. The evidence indicated that a fatal dose of arsenic had been administered at about 10 p.m. on the night of his death.

On 7 August, Margaret Rheeder was arrested and charged with the murder of her husband.

The trial, which began at the Criminal Sessions, Port Elizabeth, on 2 November, 1957, lasted eight days. Mr L.C. Barrett, the Attorney-General, was State Prosecutor. Mrs Rheeder pleaded not guilty. Despite the overwhelming body of evidence against her, she persisted in denying all accusations. At one point, she implied that her brother, Kenneth, who had visited the house on the afternoon prior to Benjamin's death, had also had the opportunity to kill her husband.

'Then are you saying the poisoner was your brother?' the Attorney-General asked.

'No. I won't say that. I will not bear false testimony.'

'Then was it one of your children?'

'No.'

'Then did your husband commit suicide?'

'No. There was no evidence to support that idea.'

'Then if it wasn't suicide and it wasn't you or any other person in the house, who was it that gave him the fatal dose?'

Mrs Rheeder paused. 'I don't know,' she said finally.

The trial was concluded on 11 November. Margaret Rheeder was found guilty of murdering her husband. In returning the verdict, the foreman of the jury requested that the court show mercy towards the accused on the grounds that she had suffered 'a hell of a life'.

The judge did not consider this an extenuating circumstance.

'Have you anything to say?' he asked before he passed the death sentence.

Mrs Rheeder was sobbing hysterically. 'My heart is too sore,' she whispered. 'I want to go to my two little children.'

'The sentence of the court,' the judge said, 'is that you be taken to a place of custody and hanged by the neck until you are dead. And may the Lord have mercy on your soul.'

In a state of near-collapse, Mrs Rheeder was helped from the court.

Margaret Rheeder declared her innocence until the very last day of her life, but as she was taken from the condemned cell to the gallows on May 6, 1957, she finally confessed to the crime for which she had been convicted.

'I cannot go to my death with a lie on my lips,' she said. 'Yes, I did give Ben the poison. The last dose was at noon in the glass of water he asked me to give him.'

This confession was not entirely true. If the fatal dose of poison had been administered at midday, Benjamin Rheeder would have been dead when Dr Bloch called at four o'clock that afternoon. It is perhaps significant that, in the course of the trial, Margaret claimed that Strydom had 'seduced' her; it transpired that he had ended their relationship three months before Ben's death. It may be that, in a final act of bitterness, she hoped to implicate Strydom – who was at home at midday – in the crime. However, the medical evidence had proved conclusively that the fatal dose of poison had been taken late at night, when she alone had had the opportunity to administer it. Indirectly, her own words had exonerated the man she wished to punish. A fitting epitaph, some would say, for the woman who talked too much.

ARSENIC is a metallic element obtained mainly from algar or orpiment ore, which are occasional by-products of lead and iron mining. Processed arsenic usually takes the form of a white powder that looks much like flour or sugar. Arsenic has been a favourite of poisoners since the eighth century, when it was first produced by an Arab alchemist. At one time, it was so popular in France that it was known as poudre de succession *or 'inheritance powder'. The symptoms of chronic arsenic poisoning – such as stomach upset, rashes and discoloration of the skin – were often attributed to other causes such as cholera and dysentery.*

Other advantages of arsenic are that it has a faintly sweet taste and it can be administered in small, cumulative doses. The victim of such dosage becomes ill, slowly deteriorates and eventually dies – a much less suspicious end than a sudden and unexpected death.

Two grains (130 mg) is recognized as a fatal dose.

12.

WIFE-KILLER

(DUNCAN DONALD MOODIE: 1961)

Duncan Moodie has the dubious distinction of being the only man in South Africa who has been tried, found guilty and sentenced to death *twice* for the same murder.

On the morning of Sunday, 21 August, 1960, Duncan Moodie, accompanied by his father, went to see his estranged wife, Anita, at her parents' home in Flora Road, Ada May Vale, Klerksdorp. He was hoping to talk his wife out of going through with the divorce for which she had recently filed. They went to speak privately in her bedroom. About twenty-five minutes later, there was a loud scream and a number of shots rang out. Moodie walked out into the hallway leaving his wife dead on the bedroom floor. She had been shot four times: twice in the head and twice in the chest.

'I didn't want to do it,' he said.

Duncan Moodie and Anita Sinclair had been sweethearts at Odendaalsrus High School, and in July 1958, they were engaged. He was twenty-three; she was nineteen.

Mr and Mrs Sinclair were against the marriage from the start. Their future son-in-law's prospects were less than encouraging: not only did he seem to find it hard to hold down a regular job, but he proved to be a heavy drinker, was often aggressive, and was becoming grossly overweight. It was hard for them to see what their daughter saw in the man, but when they realized that Anita was serious in her intention to marry Duncan, they accepted her decision with good grace. Duncan Moodie and Anita Sinclair were married on 17 January, 1959.

Things started to go wrong almost from the beginning. Moodie was subject to violent mood swings. He was lazy, violent and often out of work. But he always found enough money to buy hard liquor. Before long, he was drinking a bottle of brandy a day and began to beat his wife. Within weeks of their marriage, Anita was having to hide her bruises from her parents. When Mrs Sinclair attempted to intervene, Anita quietened her: Duncan Moodie would tolerate no interference from his in-laws.

'She's my wife,' he would say, 'and I'll do to her what I like!' This was to become his maxim.

The situation went from bad to worse, and nine months after she was married, Anita returned to her parents. A repentant Moodie stormed after her, begging her forgiveness. There was a tearful scene, after which they made up and for a couple of weeks the situation was better.

By October 1959, Duncan and Anita Moodie were deep in debt. The rent on the flat which they occupied had not been paid and a court order was issued for the repossession of their furniture. They were forced to move out and go to live with Duncan's parents in Stilfontein.

In July 1960, they moved to Durban where they hoped to make a fresh start. For a couple of weeks their relationship improved, but then Duncan returned to his old ways with a vengeance. To pay for his liquor, he pawned their few remaining valuables, including Anita's engagement ring. When he demanded her wrist-watch, she refused to give it to him; more violence followed. It was shortly after this event that she laid a charge of assault against him with the Durban police, and returned to live with her parents.

The case came to court on Monday, 15 August. Moodie was found guilty of assaulting his wife and was sentenced to three months imprisonment, suspended for three years. He was warned against molesting or committing any acts of violence against his wife during that period. By now, Anita had filed for divorce.

Moodie desperately sought a reconciliation. He followed Anita back to Klerksdorp, and telephoned her parents' house from his cousin's home. He also wrote her a long letter, proclaiming his love and promising to turn over a new leaf if only she would have him back. However, his wife remained adamant: she was going through with the divorce.

On Friday, 19 August, Moodie visited another cousin who lived in Springs. He asked to borrow a gun, which he claimed he needed in order to protect himself while he hitch-hiked across Johannesburg. He was given a pistol and five loose cartridges. He would later maintain that he had wanted the gun in order to commit suicide. That night, he booked into a Johannesburg hotel with the intention of killing himself there. The following day, he went to Johannesburg station, where he went into the mens' toilets resolved to end his life. However, 'I was too much of a coward,' he said. 'I didn't have the guts.'

It was this firearm that Moodie used to kill his wife at her parents' home the next day.

At eleven o'clock on the morning of 21 August, 1960, the Klerksdorp police were called to the Sinclairs' home. Moodie handed Lieutenant P.S. van Zyl the pistol he had used to kill his wife. The magazine and barrel were empty.

'I did not want to do it,' he repeated. 'Take me away.'

Moodie was remanded in custody awaiting trial. On 23 November, 1960, he was sent to Sterkfontein Mental Hospital for psychiatric evaluation. In late December, he escaped and made his way to Springs. Less than a day later, he surrendered to the police after contacting his parents, and shortly after that he was returned to Sterkfontein where he remained until the end of January 1961.

Moodie was brought to trial at Klerksdorp Circuit Court on 10 April, 1961.

No-one was in any doubt that Moodie had shot his wife. What was in contention, however, was his mental state at the time. Defence argued that the sequence of events preceding the tragedy at Flora Road had caused Moodie to be in such a highly-charged emotional state that he had acted automatically. For this reason, he was not responsible for his actions. The prosecution did not dispute the fact that Moodie was a psychopath, but refuted that this, in any way, excused him from the consequences of killing his wife.

After ten days of testimony, including a number of medical reports, the nine-man jury retired to the jury room to consider its verdict. Room 26 had three doors, but no windows or ventilation, and it was barely three metres by five metres. There was no table in the room, and not even enough chairs for everyone. One of the doors led out on to a street, another into the office of the Clerk of the Civil Court and the third into a passageway. The fact that the room had three doors was of great concern to the Klerksdorp Deputy-Sheriff, Mr J.H. de Wet, and to prevent the jury being interrupted during their deliberations, Mr de Wet decided to stay in the room with them. He took no part in the jury discussions and did not interfere with the proceedings in any way. The press would later label him the 'tenth man'.

After a recess, which lasted just short of two hours, the jury returned a majority verdict – guilty. Only two of the jurymen believed that there were extenuating circumstances to the murder. Before the judge, Mr Justice Snyman, passed sentence of death on Moodie, he asked him if he had anything to say.

'I only wish to say that I am glad to be able to pay my debt to society,' Moodie replied.

Moodie's attorney only learnt of the presence of the Deputy-Sheriff in the jury room the following day. He believed this to constitute a miscarriage of justice, and on 1 August, 1961, approached Mr Justice Snyman and begged leave to appeal to the Appellate Division.

The decision that was finally handed down made no criticism of the Deputy-Sheriff, Mr de Wet. Nevertheless, there had been a 'failure of justice'. Shortly afterwards, Duncan Moodie was released from prison.

Within hours of his release, he was re-arrested and charged with the same murder. In due course, he was brought before the Judge-President of the Transvaal.

'My Lord' he said, 'I have already been acquitted on this charge.'

The State refuted this claim: the Appelate Division had released Moodie on what in effect was a technicality. They had not found him not guilty. The Judge-President disagreed, saying that the State had no right to initiate further proceedings against Moodie. Once more, he was released from custody.

The State then took its case to the Appeal Court.

On 30 November, 1961, the Appeal Court overthrew the decision of the Appellate Division. It further ruled that, as a principle of law, a person cannot be *punished* or *put in jeopardy* twice for the same offence. This is not to say one cannot be *tried* twice for the same crime.

A third warrant for arrest was issued, but Moodie had already fled. After an intensive police hunt lasting ten days, he was finally apprehended at a hotel in Lobatsi in Botswana (then called Bechuanaland). He had registered in the name of D. Gordon.

Duncan Moodie's second trial for the murder of his wife, Anita, began at the Pretoria Criminal Sessions on 12 February, 1961. On this occasion, he elected to be tried by a judge and assessors rather than by jury.

Judgment was given on 21 February, 1962: Moodie was found guilty of murder and was sentenced to death a second time. Although application to appeal was denied, Moodie's father worked tirelessly over the next few months to save his son's life. (By this time the case had attracted a great deal of public sympathy, evident from the fact that a petition for clemency attracted over 25 000 signatures.)

On 28 June, 1962, after a four-week stay of execution, Duncan Moodie was hanged. It had taken twenty-two months for justice to run its full course.

13.

FOR SERVICES RENDERED

(MARTHINUS ROSSOUW: 1961)

The murder of Baron Dieter von Schauroth, who was shot to death on the night of 24 March, 1961, by his 'friend' and bodyguard, Marthinus Rossouw, is world-famous.

At the subsequent trial, Rossouw was to claim that Von Schauroth had begged to be killed. This was the first defence of its kind and would lead to a new classification of murder: *murder by request*.

Baron Dieter von Schauroth (36), who was of German descent, was from Karasburg in Namibia (formerly South West Africa). About a year before his murder, drought had forced him to sell his flock of 4 000 karakul sheep. He had moved to Cape Town with his young wife, Colleen (19). They had taken a flat in Mill Street, Gardens.

On the morning of Saturday, 25 March, 1961, Von Schauroth's body was found at the side of the Old Malmesbury Road, about 24 kilometres from Cape Town. At 7.40 a.m. Constable Jacobus Laubscher, who was stationed at Philadelphia Police Station, went to investigate a report that the body of a European male had been found close to the junction of the Old Malmesbury Road.

Von Schauroth, who was neatly dressed in green corduroy trousers and brown corduroy jacket and an open-necked, yellow and white checked shirt, was lying on his back. There was no indication that the victim's pockets had been turned out and a number of uncut diamonds were scattered around the corpse.

There were also two spent shell casings on the ground: one near the head and one near the feet. Constable Laubscher turned the body over and saw two bullet wounds in the neck just above the collar.

Von Schauroth's body was transported to Salt River mortuary where it was later identified by Detective-Constable Andries Petrus Dipenaar of the transport section. Dipenaar knew Von Schauroth, having investigated the theft of his motor car barely a month before.

On the afternoon of his murder, Von Schauroth had borrowed his sister's red Volkswagen from her home in Oranjezicht so that he could take his wife to the cinema that night. At 5.30 p.m. he had gone out 'on business'. He had told his wife to be ready when he returned at about 8 p.m. That was the last time Colleen von Schauroth saw her husband alive.

The police immediately launched an intensive investigation for the car Von Schauroth had been driving. It was found abandoned in Milnerton shortly afterwards. There was no blood in the vehicle and the keys were in the ignition.

On Monday, 27 March, three days after the murder, the police arrested Marthinus Rossouw, a twenty-three-year-old railway fitter, and charged him with the crime.

Rossouw, who was known to have been an aquaintance of Von Schauroth, lived at Hatfield House Residential Hotel in Hatfield Street, Gardens, with his wife and two small children.

Controversy surrounded the death of Von Schauroth from the outset.

There were allegations that he had been involved in illicit diamond dealing and, of course, there was the matter of his life insurance...

At a preliminary hearing held at Bellville Magistrates' Court in May 1961, it was revealed the Von Schauroth held life insurance to the value of R360 000. Dr Wilhelm Bruchner de Villiers, head of Bruchner de Villiers, insurance brokers, told the court that during the previous year Von Schauroth had taken out a number of policies through his firm. He (Von Schauroth) had insured his life for R40 000 with each of four companies and R60 000 with a fifth. In addition, on 9 December, 1960, Von Schauroth had arranged a further R140 000 in short-term life insurance which, he had claimed, was to cover a big business deal he proposed to make in May 1961. All the premiums had been paid in cash.

These revelations concerning Von Schauroth's life insurance were to assume great significance during Rossouw's trial.

The trial of Marthinus Rossouw, which was held at Cape Town Criminal Sessions in September, 1961, was presided over by Judge-President Mr Justice Beyers.

The case attracted intense public interest and hundreds of spectators swarmed into the court each day. The proceedings were also attended by the representatives of a number of major insurance companies.

In his opening address to the nine-man jury Mr W.E. Cooper, Rossouw's defence counsel, declared that his client would admit to having killed Baron von Schauroth. But there were extenuating circumstances: the whole scheme for the destruction of Von Schauroth had emanated from Von Schauroth himself. The baron, who was both unhappily married and in financial difficulties, desperately wanted to commit suicide but could not do so, since this would negate his life insurance policies. Cooper claimed that Rossouw had killed Von Schauroth as an act of deep friendship. He had, in other words, committed murder on request.

Rossouw later described how he had known Von Schauroth for a number of months and had been present when the baron had conducted illicit diamond deals. Von Schauroth had also asked him to dump his car for him at Rooi Els, letting it run down the *kranses* so that it would be damaged beyond repair. He wanted this done so that he could claim from the insurance company for the loss of his car. Rossouw also maintained that on a number of occasions Von Schauroth had offered him R10 000 to kill 'someone'.

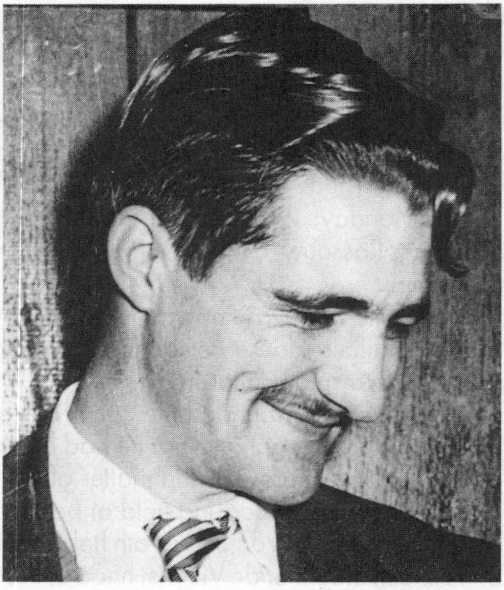

Photograph courtesy of *Die Burger*

Marthinus Rossouw

'I once asked him who he wanted shot,' Rossouw explained, 'and he laughed and said possibly his wife, his mother-in-law, Mr Nel (a business associate) or even his child.'

On the night preceding Von Schauroth's murder, Rossouw and the baron had gone to the Avalon Hotel for a drink together. According to Rossouw, Von Schauroth had said, 'Colleen is in a temper again tonight.'

'He often told me he was very unhappy because of his wife,' Rossouw would add later. 'He had found out she was going out with other men. I knew his wife before I got married. I used to go to night clubs and saw her there in the company of men. I came to the conclusion she was not a decent girl.'

At the time of the murder, Rossouw was negotiating to buy a motorcar but was short of cash. Von Schauroth offered to give him the R80 he needed to pay the deposit. He also reminded Rossouw that he would give him R10 000 if he would kill 'someone'. Afterwards, the baron gave him a lift home. In the car, outside Rossouw's apartment, Von Schauroth gave Rossouw a cheque for R2 300 for 'services rendered'. The cheque, which Von Schauroth had previously received from his late brother, was post-dated 3 July, 1962.

'Why did he give you the cheque?' the Judge asked.

'He said he would give me the cheque if I accompanied him as his bodyguard,' Rossouw replied.

The following night, Rossouw met Von Schauroth at Cape Town station at 5 p.m. They went first to the Prince of Wales Hotel and then drove out to the Cambridge Hotel in Milnerton. Their final stop for the night was at Killarney, where they had one more drink. They then headed along the Old Malmesbury Road. While we were driving [the baron] reminded me that I was to shoot someone for him and said: "It might be tonight'. He also said there were a few diamonds in his pocket but that they were not very valuable. He sang a German song then became very serious. He said that he was unhappy with his wife and tired of life. Then he laughed, clapped me on the shoulder and said, "Everything will come right, Marthinus". Then he leaned over the back of the car and picked up a raincoat. He took out a pistol and put the coat on the floor between us.

'At the Old Malmesbury Road he told me to stop. I stopped the car facing the national road. He then gave me the revolver and two boxes of cartridges. He loaded the revolver with two cartridges, using a handkerchief. He then got out and walked to the spot where the body was found. I thought he was trying to frighten me. He then turned round and said, "Marthiens, I want you to shoot me." I said, "No, it is too dangerous." He pleaded with me and said there were no witnesses and that it would look like a diamond transaction. He said he could not commit suicide or his wife would not be able to collect the insurance money. He again turned his back on me and said, "Please, Marthiens, shoot me." I replied, 'No, Dieter, I cannot.'

He pleaded with me for five or ten minutes. He said he wanted to go to a place where there were no women. He then turned around and we shook hands. He said that his bank manager would give me R10 000. He said, '*Tot siens*, Marthiens.'

'I then shot him. He had told me to shoot him in the back of the neck. He jerked with the first shot then I shot him again. He turned as I shot him. I shot him because I felt sorry for him. He was unhappy with his wife. His wife had a reputation and his mother-in-law...'

Afterwards, Rossouw abandoned Von Schauroth's car in Milnerton and caught a bus home. He went to bed, but later rose and went to Sea Point, where he threw the gun and the cartridges into the sea. He finally got back to his flat at about 12.45 a.m.

When the police questioned Rossouw the following day, he denied having seen Von Schauroth on the night of his murder. On Monday, he went to collect his new car at Fredman Motors where the police were waiting for him and he was arrested.

During the trial, Mr van den Berg, the Attorney-General, disputed both Rossouw's alleged motive for the killing and his account of the actual murder. He maintained that Rossouw had killed Von Schauroth simply for the R2 300 cheque. (At the time of the murder Rossouw was short of money and his rental was a month in arrears.) Rossouw strongly denied these allegations.

'I killed him because he was tired of life,' he said.

'Did you not say to him, "You have such a bad wife, why do you want to kill yourself to enrich her?" the judge asked.

'Well, he was unhappy, but he still loved his wife.'

Mr van den Berg also threw doubt on Rossouw's description of the murder. A forensic expert testified that it was unlikely that Von Schauroth had been killed in exactly the way Rossouw described, since victims who are shot in the back of the neck inevitably fall forward. A further complication was the fact that the two cartridge cases had been found in different places.

'I cannot exclude the possibility,' the expert said, 'that after one shot had been fired, the second shot had been fired into the back of the neck as the body lay on the ground.'

By the time Rossouw came to court, he had changed his story twice, and under questioning he proved to be less than reliable. He could not explain, for example, how the diamonds which were found around Von Schauroth's body came to be on the ground. He denied scattering them himself. 'It must have been the baron,' he said.

On 27 September, 1961, the jury retired to consider its verdict. After less than an hour, they returned a verdict of guilty with no extenuating circumstances.

Marthinus Rossouw was hanged at Pretoria Central Prison on 20 June, 1962. He had shared the condemned cell with Duncan Donald Moodie, who was later to hang for the murder of his wife, Anita. When Rossouw was called, the two men embraced, then Rossouw was led away to the gallows singing *Nearer my God to Thee*.

During his last few hours, Rossouw wrote out a last will and testament in which he left the R2 300 which Von Schauroth had paid him to his family. One thousand rand was to go to his widow and R400 each to his two children, Gabriel and Wilhelmina.

14. DEATH IN PARLIAMENT

(1966)

Hendrik Frensch Verwoerd, psychologist, sociologist, journalist, statesman and the architect of *apartheid*, was born in Amsterdam on 8 September, 1901. He was, as he bluntly admitted in 1947, 'an extreme Afrikaner'.

In 1925, he obtained a doctorate at Stellenbosch University and then went to America and Europe, where he did post-graduate studies at a number of universities, including Hamburg and Berlin. In 1928, he returned to South Africa and was appointed Professor of Applied Psychology and Sociology at Stellenbosch University.

In 1936, he joined a deputation of six professors in protesting against the admission to South Africa of Jewish refugees from Nazi Germany. From that year on, Dr Verwoerd was destined to be surrounded by controversy.

In 1937, he became the first editor of *Die Transvaler*, the National Party newspaper in Johannesburg. Under his editorship, *Die Transvaler* became an extremist organ, strenuously voicing its opposition to the Hertzog-Smuts alliance and to South Africa's involvement in World War II. A Supreme Court judgment against Verwoerd would later hold that *Die Transvaler* made a tool of the Nazis in South Africa; and he knew it.

In 1948, the National Party swept to power in the general election. Dr Verwoerd's contribution to the party's success was clearly recognized and he was elected to the Senate, where he became the leader of the ruling party. Two years later, he entered the Cabinet and was appointed Minister of Native Affairs. It was shortly after this appointment that Dr Verwoerd declared that the National Party had developed a policy '... which grants to others what it claims for itself and which is calculated to provide the same opportunities to everyone within his own race group. That is the policy of *apartheid*'.

On 2 September, 1958, after the death of J.G. Strijdom, Dr Verwoerd became Prime Minister.

The year 1960 was a dramatic one for South African politics and for Verwoerd personally. In January, he announced that a referendum would be called to determine the republican issue; the object would be a republic within the British Commonwealth. Two weeks later, Harold Macmillan, the then British

Prime Minister, visited South Africa. In an address to both Houses of Parliament he made his famous 'winds of change' speech and criticised *apartheid*. On 21 March, 1960, there was Sharpeville. Then, less than a month later, the first attempt to assassinate Dr Verwoerd almost succeeded.

On 9 April, 1960, Dr Verwoerd opened the Union Exposition on the Witwatersrand to mark the jubilee of the Union of South Africa.

Having made his opening speech, he took his seat. Shortly afterwards, a fifty-two year-old farmer, David Pratt, walked up to him and fired two shots into his face. The police later gave the following account of the incident:

'After Verwoerd had made his opening speech, a man stepped up near to the front row of seats in which the Prime Minister was sitting.

'Some versions are that the man drew attention to himself by calling out, "Dr Verwoerd". Other onlookers did not hear the Prime Minister's name being called.

'A shot was fired at virtually point-blank range into Dr Verwoerd's right cheek from a .22 automatic pistol. A second shot was fired into his right ear.

'Col. G.M. Harrison, president of the Witwatersrand Agricultural Society, leapt up and knocked the pistol from the gunman's hand. After the pistol fell to the floor, Colonel Harrison, with the help of Major (Carl) Richter (the Prime Minister's personal bodyguard), civilians and another policeman overpowered the gunman and hustled him to the showgrounds Police Station.

'The arrest was made so quickly and the removal was done so quickly that an angry section of the crowd was frustrated from assaulting the detainee.

'The detainee, David Pratt, was soon thereafter hurried to Marshall Square.'

Within minutes of the assassination attempt, Dr Verwoerd was rushed – still conscious – to the Pretoria Hospital. Two days later, the hospital issued a statement which described his condition as 'indeed satisfactory – further examinations were carried out today and they confirm good expectations. Dr Verwoerd at present is restful. There is no need for any immediate operation.'

The surgeons who worked on Dr Verwoerd would later claim that his escape had been 'absolutely miraculous'. One specialist declared that the firearm used '... could not have been anything bigger than a .22 bullet without causing very much more damage.'

Other physicians agreed that if a larger calibre gun had been used, the bullet would probably have penetrated the temple bone and lodged in the brain with extremely serious consequences.

Specialist surgeons were called in to remove the bullets. At first, there was speculation that Dr Verwoerd would lose his hearing and sense of balance, but these fears were to prove groundless. He returned to public life on 29 May, less than two months after the shooting.

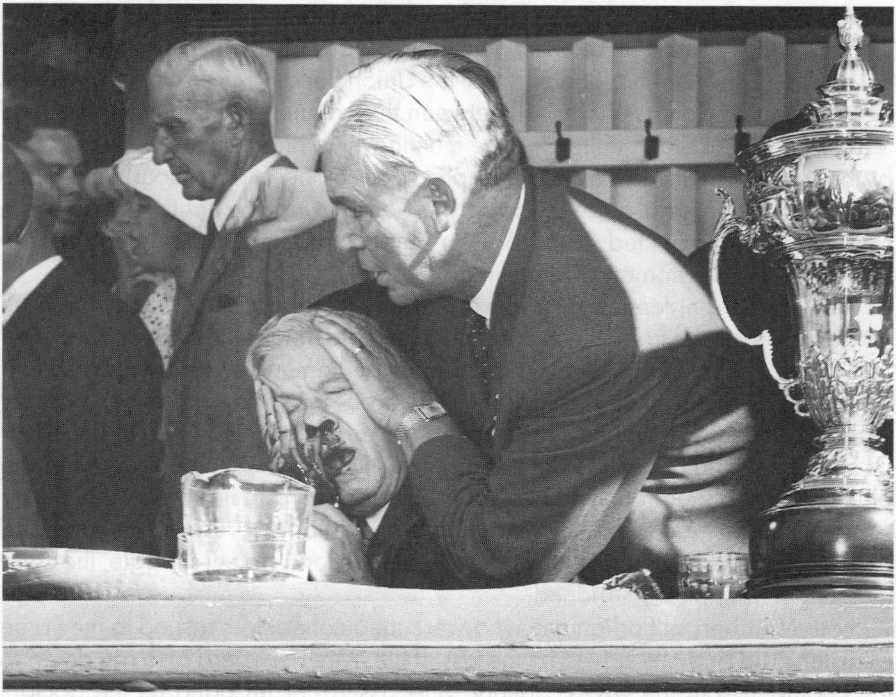

Photograph by kind permission J. J. Wesselo

Verwoerd after the first assassination attempt

David Pratt, Dr Verwoerd's would-be assassin, appeared in the Johannesburg Magistrates' Court on 11 April. Pratt was the father of three who had suffered from epilepsy for a number of years. He was described as a 'socialite and farmer'. He was a respected member of the Witwatersrand Agricultural Society and had been close to Dr Verwoerd on a number of occasions prior to the shooting. In fact, it was later revealed that Pratt had been one of the VIPs sitting near to Dr Verwoerd during the opening of the exposition.

David Pratt, who claimed he had been shooting 'the epitome of *apartheid*', was eventually declared 'mentally disordered and epileptic'. On 26 September, 1960, he was committed to Pretoria Central Prison to 'await indication of the Governor General's pleasure'. On 1 October, 1961, he hanged himself at Bloemfontein Mental Hospital.

Dr Verwoerd had escaped death by a hair's breadth. Six years later, he would not be so fortunate.

On 6 September, 1966, an air of expectancy hung over Parliament.

Three days earlier, Dr Verwoerd had held historic talks with the Prime Minister of Lesotho, Chief Leabua Johnathan, at the Union Buildings in Pretoria. It was the first meeting on South African soil between the premier of South Africa and the leader of a black state. Following the meeting, a joint communique was issued by the two governments with special emphasis on co-operation without interference in each others' internal affairs. Against this background, the South African Prime Minister was expected to make an important policy statement at the parliamentary session on 6 September.

Dr Verwoerd entered the House of Assembly that day at 2.15 p.m.. As he made his way to the front bench, he exchanged greetings with those around him. Just as he was taking his seat, a uniformed parliamentary messenger, Dimitri Tsafendas, walked briskly across the floor from the lobby entrance. Without warning, Tsafendas drew a sheath knife from under his clothing. He bent over Dr Verwoerd and raised his right hand high into the air. With his left hand, he plucked off the sheath and then stabbed Dr Verwoerd four times in the chest.

Seconds later, a number of Members of Parliament rushed forward and pulled Tsafendas away from the Prime Minister. After a violent struggle, the court messenger was finally subdued.

Four Members of Parliament who were medical doctors rushed to the Prime Minister's aid and one gave him the kiss-of-life. Mrs Verwoerd also ran down to the chamber from the wives' gallery. She kissed her husband as the doctors battled to save his life. The Prime Minister was rushed to Groote Schuur Hospital where he was certified dead-on-arrival.

On 17 October, 1966, a summary trial for Tsafendas began. It ended three days later, with the declaration by Justice Beyers that Tsafendas was 'insane and unfit to stand trial'. Beyers ordered that Tsafendas 'be kept in a place of safety where he will be away from society' and he was confined to Pretoria Central Prison.

Tsafendas, who was 48 years-old at the time of the assassination, is the son of a Cypriot father and a black Mozambique mother, but is classified as white.

Tsafendas has a history of mental illness which goes back to 1935.

He has been diagnosed as suffering from paranoid schizophrenia, in particular, a persistent delusion that a giant tapeworm is eating him up from inside.

Only one interview with Tsafendas has ever been published: it appeared in the *Citizen* newspaper in 1976. In it, Tsafendas maintained that he was being well treated in prison and was receiving regular psychiatric treatment. He also pointed out that he was allowed extra helpings of carrots, since that particular vegetable helped with the tapeworm.

It was later learnt that the *Citizen* interviewer, Gordon Winter, was a government agent working for the Bureau of State Security. Winter would later claim in his book, *Inside BOSS*, that the motivation for the interview was to defuse claims of alleged ill-treatment made by Brian Price, an alleged drug dealer, in *The Observer*.

On 30 September, 1989, Dimitri Tsafendas was transferred from Pretoria Central Prison to Zonderwater Prison near Cullinan.

Technically, only the State President can order his release.

15.

THE GLAZER KIDNAPPING

(1966)

On 30 March, 1966, South Africa was again in the news. This time as a result of a kidnapping.

Mrs Etty Glazer, the wife of well-known Johannesburg multi-millionaire, Bernard Glazer, was kidnapped with her 22-month-old son, Sammy, after dropping off her two daughters at junior school. The ransom subsequently demanded was R140 000, which was four times as much as the US $50 000 paid in the famous Lindbergh kidnapping, until that time the highest ransom demand in the world.

The police learnt of the kidnapping by accident, yet, within two weeks of the crime, the four men responsible were apprehended and most of the money returned. The then Minister of Justice, John Vorster, issued a special statement at the time which read: 'The full story of the investigation reads like a work of fiction. If there is a detective force in the world that can do better, I should like to hear of it.'

At about eight o'clock on the morning of 30 March, Mrs Glazer left her Morningside home in a station wagon to take her two daughters, Michelle (7) and Ella (5) to Sandown Public School. She was wearing her dressing-gown over her nightclothes. Having dropped off the two girls, she headed back home. On an open gravel road about half a mile from her home, she saw a car parked on the left-hand side of the road; the boot and the bonnet of the car were open. Two men were standing in the road alongside the car and a third man was sitting inside the car. They appeared to be having car trouble. As she approached, one of the men stepped on to the road in front of her car and flagged her down. When she stopped, he walked around to the driver's side window and without warning grabbed hold of her arm. 'This is security,' he said. On the other side of the car his accomplice tried to get inside but the doors were locked. Realizing that something was terribly wrong, Mrs Glazer began to scream for help and sounded the hooter. Moments later, the two men were inside. There was a brief struggle, during which the hooter was broken and Mrs Glazer's lip was cut, then she was subdued. Both she and the child were hysterical.

'What do you want of me?' she asked.

'We are political refugees. We need your car,' one of the men replied.

'Then take my car and leave me,' she said.

'We need you too,' they answered.

Having been forced out of the driving seat, she was told to lie down on the floor of the car, but refused. One of the kidnappers then pulled out a gun. 'Behave and act normally,' he warned.

Before they moved off, the second kidnapper removed Mrs Glazer's spectacles. Then he held his hands over her eyes throughout the short journey that followed. When they arrived at the house where she was to be held, they turned off the road and pulled into a garage, where, once the doors had been closed, she was allowed to see. She had no idea where she was.

Mrs Glazer and her son were then taken into the house, where she was ordered to contact her husband. One of the men said, 'We want £70 000 for your release.'

Mrs Glazer's husband was *en route* to Swaziland and it was impossible to contact him, so her first phone call was to her mother, to whom she explained her predicament, and that the kidnappers wanted R140 000 for her release. She also warned her mother not to tell the police or anyone else. Next, she phoned her husband's secretary, Mr Davis.

Soon after the conversation had ended, Davis set out for Swaziland.

When Mr Glazer heard the news, he immediately returned to Johannesburg where his mother-in-law was waiting for him at his home.

At 6 p.m. Mr Glazer spoke to his wife. Afterwards, a man came to the phone. 'Mr Glazer,' he said, 'we want £70 000 for your son's and wife's release. If you want your wife and child alive you must pay £70 000 – and Mr Glazer, no tricks, no marked money and no police if you want your wife and child alive.'

Mr Glazer explained that he had to go to Pretoria to get the money. He then contacted the manager of his bank and arranged to withdraw the cash – all in R10 and R20 notes – after hours. He reached the bank at about 11 p.m., where he was met by a bank official. The man allowed him to withdraw the R140 000 he needed, but not before he made a list of the numbers of certain of the notes.

Mr Glazer received another telephone call at his home that night. This time, he was given explicit instructions concerning the handing-over of the money. He was to drive to Corlett Drive and park his car at bus-stop 50. He was to wait at the telephone booth there for further instructions. Mr Glazer did exactly as he was told. He was ordered to leave the money on the back seat of the car and the doors unlocked. He was to go for a walk down the street. He did so, and when he returned to the car, the money had gone.

At 2 a.m. Mr Glazer received another phone call informing him that his wife and son were to be released and would be home in half an hour. Shortly after this, the kidnappers took Mrs Glazer and her son for a drive. Some distance from the house where she had been held, they jumped out of the station wagon and sped away in their own vehicle. Mrs Glazer then drove herself home. Fortunately, neither she nor her son had been molested in any way, and they were physically unharmed.

In the meantime, the police had found out all about the kidnapping. They had been alerted to the situation by Mr Glazer's bank manager, who was alarmed when his client had demanded to withdraw such a large amount cash 'under mysterious circumstances' late at night. (Mr Glazer had insisted that the bank be opened so that he could withdraw R140 000 for which amount he issued a cheque. He was clearly in an extremely agitated state, but would not say why he so desperately needed the money.) The head of the security police, Brigadier Hendrick van den Bergh, had moved swiftly once the matter had been brought to his attention. He arrived at the Glazer mansion just as Mr Glazer returned home after paying the ransom. Although he forced Mr Glazer to reveal what was happening, Mr Glazer refused to allow the police to act until his wife and son had been released.

The following morning, Jannie Nel, at that time a sergeant in the South African Crime Bureau (but later news editor of the *Rand Daily Mail*) was sworn to secrecy and taken to meet Mrs Glazer at her home.

His task was to draw up a detailed plan of the house in which she had been kept prisoner, in the hope that the place could be traced.

When Sergeant Nel first met Mrs Glazer, she was still in a state of shock after her ordeal, but slowly he asked his questions. Eventually, Mrs Glazer drew what she thought was a rough outline of the house, but what Nel would later describe as little more than an 'elaborate squiggle'. Three days later, however, the elaborate squiggle had transformed into a detailed master plan which would play a significant role in the capture of the kidnappers.

'She began the debriefing almost a total wreck, but by the end was able to give remarkable details about the inside of the kidnap house,' said Nel.

The police had three more useful pieces of information to help in the search. During the kidnap, one of the kidnappers had sent a telegram to Israel at Mrs Glazer's request; it was traced to the Bramley area. The kidnappers had also bought a dummy and some food for Sammy, Mrs Glazer's son, from a Bramley pharmacist. And Mrs Glazer estimated that the house to which she had been taken was 'about two miles away [from the scene of the abduction] as the crow flies'. In this way, the police were able to narrow down their search.

Eventually, detailed copies of the 'master plan' were duplicated and distributed to 500 hand-picked policemen, who were all from Pretoria so as to ensure total security. The men were sent out with the maps, instructed to pose as telephone personnel, and ordered to visit the 6 000 houses in the Bramley area. The house which had been used in the kidnapping was discovered on the first day. It belonged to one Leonard Landau Levy (43).

Leonard Levy was immedicately identified by Mrs Glazer as one of the men who had held her captive. When he was confronted by the police, he denied any involvement in the kidnapping. However, he did admit that on a date prior to the kidnapping, he had been approached by his brother Ephraim (39) and a friend, Stanley Ivan Jawitz (36), to lend them his house for seven days; he would be paid R10 000 for the favour. Leonard Levy claimed that he had first refused, but agreed to lend the two men his house on 29 March, the day before the kidnapping.

Leonard Levy later took police to a building society in Johannnesburg, where there was a safe-deposit box containing R6 990, which he handed over. The police then arrested Ephraim Levy at his Bantry Bay home in Cape Town and recovered a further R58 500 from him. On the morning of April 13, the police recovered R60 000 from a safe-deposit box belonging to Stanley Jawitz.

On the previous evening, Jawitz, who was being questioned by the police, had committed suicide by jumping to his death from the top of an apartment block in Berea, Johannesburg.

Kenneth, the third Levy brother, was also implicated in the crime and arrested by the police.

The trial of Ephraim, Leonard and Kenneth Levy, all of whom were accused of kidnapping and child stealing, began at the Rand Supreme Court on 1 June, 1966. The presiding judge was Mr Justice Hiemstra.

All three men initially pleaded not guilty, but on the second day of the trial, Ephraim Levy changed his plea to guilty. He was tried separately from his two brothers.

On 10 June, all three brothers were convicted of kidnapping. Ephraim Levy was sentenced to 16 years in jail, Kenneth to 6 years and Leonard to 5 years. They were denied leave to appeal.

Throughout the trial Kenneth Levy maintained that he was not involved in the kidnapping, despite the fact that, apart from other things, he had been driving the car used in the abduction of Mrs Glazer.

'I was recovering from a motor-car accident at the time,' Levy maintained. 'I had sustained serious head injuries and had suffered brain haemorrhage – I did not even know my own name – how on earth could I have known that I was being drawn into a kidnapping?'

Mr Justice Hiemstra, however, was convinced of Levy's guilt. At the summing up he declared: 'You [Kenneth] were an active participant to a greater extent than your brother Leonard. You were on the scene of the kidnapping and knew what was going on. You saw fit to deny that you knew anything about it and by so doing forfeited much of the compassion one could have had for you in your present predicament.'

Bernard Glazer instituted a civil action against Kenneth Levy for the return of the missing ransom money. In June 1967, the Rand Supreme Court ordered Levy to pay Glazer R2 500. Ephraim and Leonard Levy, whose estates had been sequestrated in the interim, were exonerated from liability.

The Glazer Kidnapping, written by Kenneth Levy in collaboration with his journalist nephew, Barry Levy, was published in 1986. In it, Levy professes his innocence in the affair and says that he was dragged into the intrigue by Stanley Jawitz, whom he hero-worshipped. Jawitz's suicide ensured that facts which would have exonerated him, never came to light.

One of the most famous kidnapping cases at that time involved the infant son of the famous aviator, Charles Lindbergh (the first man to cross the Atlantic Ocean by aeroplane; he made the flight in his own Spirit of St Louis). The child was kidnapped on 1 March, 1932, from the Lindbergh's New Jersey home.

The kidnapper, who used a ladder to gain access to the child's bedroom, left a ransom note for $50 000. This figure was later raised to $70 000. Dr John Condon, a friend of the Lindbergh family, offered his services as mediator. After weeks of delays and setbacks, Condon eventually met a man named John in the Bronx. In exchange for $50 000 'John' told him that the missing child was to be found on board a boat by the name of Nellie at Martha's Vineyard near Massachusetts.

This information turned out to be false. In May 1932, the body of the child was discovered about five miles from the Lindbergh's house; the infant boy had been killed by a blow to the head and had been dead for about two months. His murderer was never traced.

Possibly the most famous kidnapping of recent years is that of Eugene Paul Getty II, the seventeen-year old grandson of billionaire Paul Getty.

On 10 July, 1973, Getty was kidnapped in Rome. His mother, the former actress Gail (Getty) Harris, soon received a telephone ransom demand for $17-million.

Paul Getty senior stated that he refused, on principle, to pay any ransom.

In November 1973, an envelope was delivered to the Rome daily newspaper, Il Messaggero. *It contained a lock of reddish hair and a severed human ear. An accompanying typed message read: 'This is Paul's first ear. If within 10 days the family still believes this is a joke mounted by him, then the other ear will arrive. In other words, he will arrive in little bits.'*

Eventually, Paul Getty senior capitulated and a ransom thought to be in the region of R2,8-million was paid.

Paul Getty was released, minus his ear, in mid-December 1973.

16.

MURDER WITH A BLUNT INSTRUMENT

(RONALD COHEN: 1970)

A murder trial which attracted immense public interest, both at home and overseas, was that of millionaire Ronald Vivien Cohen, who battered his wife to death at their fashionable Constantia home on the evening of 5 April, 1970. The motive for the killing was never established.

Ronald Cohen and Susan Jonson were married on 26 February, 1963. He was thirty-four, a rich and successful businessman, and she was eighteen. It was his second marriage, his first having ended in divorce five years earlier.

In 1967, Cohen bought two acres of land on 'millionaire's row' – Monterey Drive, Southern Cross, Constantia – for R12 000. The magnificent Spanish-Moorish-type house he had built there was named *Southcape*.

On 30 March, 1970, Susan Cohen took their two children, Jonathan (3) and Jaquiline (1), to the Wilderness for a week's holiday. Cohen himself was not able to go with them due to business pressures, but he spoke to his wife on numerous occasions during the week. His marriage, he said, was 'extremely happy'.

On the afternoon of 5 April, Cohen picked up his family at D.F. Malan airport in Cape Town and returned to *Southcape* at around 7 p.m. Half an hour later, Susan telephoned her father. She seemed to be happy, Mr Jonson said, and was 'glad to be back'.

After the children had been put to bed, Ronald and Susan had supper in the library. At about 10.30 p.m., Cohen left the library to go to the toilet and was away, he claimed, for about ten minutes. As he opened the door of the library, on his return, he saw his wife struggling with an intruder. The man, he said, was blond, about 27 to 29 years-old, with a V-shaped face, hollow cheeks and dressed in light sportswear.

'They were both facing me,' he said. 'He had his arm around her shoulders and was hitting her about the head with a white object. My wife had her arms stretched out towards me and was screaming.

'I rushed over towards them and tried to grapple with him. I found difficulty in getting at him as she was between us. In her desperation to get away she grappled with me.

'I do remember, vaguely, that I got him on the shoulder. Out of the corner of my eye I saw on a little table standing next to the settee, a bronze (ram's head) ornament. I grabbed it and lifted it up with the intention of hitting this man with it. From that time on I don't remember what happened. My next recollection was rising up towards the man. He was holding the heavy stone ornament with both his hands. I lifted up my hands and grabbed it.'

Cohen noticed that the man was wearing brown gloves and then blacked out. The next thing he knew was that he was kneeling on the floor beside his wife and 'seeing this frightful spectacle of her head... the terrible injuries'.

In another wing of the house, Yvonne Merry, the Cohen's housemaid was in bed. Just before eleven o'clock, she heard four or five dull thuds then, after a pause, a few more. She assumed the thuds were caused by a door banging on the far side of the house. Shortly afterwards, she heard Cohen shouting for her and seconds later he burst into her room and switched on the light.

'Come quickly,' he shouted, 'someone's broken in...'

She followed him to the library and saw Mrs Cohen lying on the floor. The library door which led out on to a terrace was open. Cohen, who was visibly shaken and apparently in great distress, was kneeling next to his wife. A few moments later, he got to his feet.

'She has been murdered,' he said. 'Call the police. I am going to get my gun and I am going out.'

Shortly after 11 p.m., Pinelands police control received an emergency telephone call from Cohen himself.

'Please send the police,' he gasped. 'My wife has been murdered, murdered, MURDERED...'.

The police arrived at *Southcape* less than ten minutes later where Cohen met them at the front door. He had blood on his shirt and there were bruises and scratches on his arms. They found Mrs Cohen lying dead in the library. Her head was shattered and there was a massive wound over her right ear and temple, through which broken pieces of bone protruded. Rigor mortis had not yet set in. Near to the body lay the bronze cast of a ram's head, which weighed approximately three-and-a-half kilograms and a stone statuette. The articles, both of which had been wedding presents, were bloodstained.

Just after midnight, Lieutenant Floris Johannes Mostert, the head of the Murder and Robbery Squad, arrived at *Southcape*. Cohen described to him the sequence of events as he recalled them, but was vague on a number of key points. This made Lieutenant Mostert suspicious, particularly the fact that Cohen's recollection of the incident was extremely fragmentary from the point at which he grappled with the intruder. He couldn't say whether the intruder had hit him, or knocked him out, yet he could give a detailed description of the man. 'He was smiling,' Cohen said, 'like he was enjoying himself.'

At about 2 a.m., Cohen was examined by the Wynberg District Surgeon, who found no evidence of a blow to the head.

In the early hours of 6 April, Cohen was arrested and charged with the murder of his wife. He was later released on R10 000 bail.

As the court date approached, public interest began to grow to fever pitch. Then, on 2 July, there occurred yet another startling development.

On the morning of 2 July, Cohen visited the tailoring department of Markham's in Cape Town, where he had a suit fitting at about 11 a.m. As he was leaving the shop by the Hout Street entrance, he claimed he glimpsed his wife's murderer on the opposite pavement. The killer, he said, was wearing a hat and carrying a blue airline bag. He immediately gave chase, but lost the man in Adderley Street.

Photograph courtesy of *Die Burger*

Ronald Cohen

'If there was any doubt in my mind,' Cohen would later state at his trial, 'it was removed by the fact that when he saw me, he started to run.'

This story, however, was not confirmed by two Markham's tailors who had watched Cohen walk down the street after he left the shop. According to them, he neither ran nor shouted nor showed any sign of agitation. Nor did they see a man with a hat and a blue airline bag.

A few days after this incident, Cohen placed an advertisement in a number of national newspapers. Under the heading *'Do you know this man?'* was a portrait, drawn by a local artist, of the man who had reputedly broken into *Southcape* on the night of 5 April. A R5 000 reward was offered to anyone who could give information leading to the identification of the killer, but no-one responded to the advertisement.

The trial of Ronald Cohen began at the Cape Town Criminal Sessions on 24 August, 1970, with Mr Justice Beyers presiding.

During his opening address, Mr A.J. Lategan, who represented the State, conceded that the prosecution had a difficult task to prove beyond reasonable doubt that Ronald Cohen had murdered his wife. However, as he pointed out, the circumstances surrounding the crime allowed for no other conclusion but that Cohen was guilty.

Firstly, Cohen's claim that an intruder had entered the house and murdered his wife did not stand up to close scrutiny since there was neither 'spoor' nor 'trace' of the alleged killer. There was absolutely no evidence of a break-in. Secondly, there was no motive for the intruder to have entered the house: nothing was missing from the library and there was no indication whatsoever of a sexual assault on Mrs Cohen. And thirdly, the fact that the accused claimed to remember only certain unrelated details of the crime went against medical experience.

Cohen recalled seeing his wife in the clutches of the man – but could not remember being struck on the head. In fact, there was no evidence to suggest that Cohen had been hit on the head at all. He also recalled the assailant's expression and that he was wearing brown gloves – but could not identify the 'white object' which he claimed the man was carrying. Cohen also remembered picking up the bronze statue at one point – but didn't know what happened after that. Nor could he remember what he thought as he knelt over his wife after the intruder had departed.

These 'islands of memory', as they came to be known, were to become a controversial aspect of Cohen's trial for murder.

Dr J.C. de Villiers, a neurosurgeon at Groote Schuur Hospital, maintained that it was 'impossible' to have 'two amnesias' as a consequence of the type of light head injury Cohen received. 'Islands of memory,' he pointed out to the court, 'were associated with cases where head injuries are "severe" or "moderate'"and where there was a long period of "blacking out".

Dr de Villiers also added that any head injury which is severe enough to cause a loss of consciousness results in retrograde amnesia which blots out the memory of the traumatic occurrence. This type of built-in protection prevents repeated recollection of a painful event.

By claiming to recall only certain aspects of the night in question, Cohen unwittingly undermined his own defence and caused his account of the murder to lose credibility.

On 18 September, Ronald Cohen was found guilty of murdering his wife. As judgment was passed, Cohen leaned forward to where his father sat on the bench in front of the dock and patted him on the hand. Afterwards, looking pale but calm, he was led down to the cells.

Justice Beyers passed sentence on 21 September, after a weekend of 'very hard thinking'.

'I have no wish to prolong the agony,' he began on the Monday morning. 'I have thought hard and I have no intention of passing the death sentence in this case. This is a case in which I feel the death sentence is not the appropriate one....'

Furthermore, he added, the whole tragedy would be even more tragic if the extreme penalty was demanded, since there were extenuating circumstances. Cohen appeared to have killed his wife in a moment of *diminished responsibility*, a conclusion which the facts supported as there was no indication of premediatation about the crime.

'I am satisfied,' Justice Beyers concluded, 'that Cohen committed the crime during a period of diminished responsibility.'

Ronald Cohen was sentenced to twelve years in prison.

■

After serving five years of his sentence, Ronald Cohen was released on parole on 21 September, 1975. He returned to live in Cape Town where he was received by Mr and Mrs Jonson, his late wife's parents, who had looked after his two children during his absence.

'I am eternally grateful to Mr and Mrs Jonson, whom I love dearly,' he declared. 'I am thankful for everything they have done for my children and for their help in the last few years. Under the circumstances, it must have been hard for them.'

The term 'diminished responsibility' implies that the accused was suffering from an abnormality of the mind which impaired judgement at the time the offence was committed. If pleaded successfully, a charge of murder is reduced to one of culpable homicide.

17.

THE GREAT TRUST BANK ROBBERY (1971)

In a daring raid on 28 April, 1971, a security van containing over R240 000 was taken from outside the Commissioner Street branch of the Trust Bank in Johannesburg. At the time, it was the biggest bank robbery in South African history and one which the South African press was comparing to the biggest robberies of them all: the theft of over R7-million worth of German national gold reserves by American military personnel and German civilians in 1945, and the Great Train robbery in Britain, in 1963, which netted R5-million.

But, what is perhaps even more amazing about the crime is that it was planned and executed, not by professional thieves, but by two complete amateurs. Derek Whitehead and Willem Antonie van der Merwe, both aged thirty, were painting contractors who decided to rob a bank in order to solve their firm's financial difficulties. When the two robbers finally counted their loot, they were surprised to discover just how much money they had stolen.

In 1968, Whitehead and Van der Merwe became partners in a painting business. For over a year, the firm did well until about the middle of 1970, when things took a turn for the worse. At first, the idea of robbing a bank was simply a joke, but when things got to the stage where they couldn't pay their domestic accounts, it was no longer a laughing matter.

'We were absolutely desperate,' Whitehead would later admit.

At the beginning of 1971, the two men decided that their best option was to sell their houses in Johannesburg, buy ground on the Garden Route, and build holiday cottages together.

With this plan in mind, Whitehead and Van der Merwe drove to Knysna to look at plots. It was while they were travelling to the coast that it suddenly occurred to them how easy it would be to break into some of the small-town banks that they passed. The idea quickly took root and by the time the two men returned to Johannesburg, they had already made serious plans. In March of the same year, they acquired cutting equipment and tools and an accomplice by the name of Gilbert Mthembu and set out once more. This time their destination was Uniondale in the Cape Province.

Around dawn, the three of them smashed a window at the back of the Uniondale branch of the Volkskas Bank and entered the building. Then, realising that it would soon be daylight and that the locals would be up and about, they reluctantly abandoned the attempt and set out for Knysna.

The next day, they considered a renewed attempt but couldn't pluck up sufficient courage to break in and decided to head back to the Transvaal. *En route* they stopped at Aberdeen and attempted to rob the Volkskas Bank there. While Whitehead kept watch at the front, Van der Merwe and Mthembu entered the bank through a back window. Fifteen minutes later they were back at the car. As it turned out, the safe was made of carbon steel and was resistant to cutting torches.

Back in Johannesburg, the Trust Bank repossessed the cars Whitehead and Van der Merwe were using, and the two men finally decided to close down their business. Ironically, it was while Van der Merwe was discussing the situation with a bank official at the Hillbrow branch of the Trust Bank that the idea of stealing a security van first occurred to him. He saw some money being brought in and was amazed at the security firm's negligence in that its vehicle was left unattended outside the bank for over fifteen minutes.

For some days after that Van der Merwe followed the security van.

'We noticed that the van regularly called at the Fox Street branch after being at the Reserve Bank,' Whitehead explained. 'We knew that if we obtained keys to the van it would be simple to drive off with it as it was left unguarded in front of the bank.'

The problem was how to obtain the keys to the vehicle, but this proved much easier to solve than either of them expected. After giving the matter some thought, the two men decided to cause the van to break down, follow it to the garage where it was sent to be repaired, and try to obtain duplicates there.

On the night of 25 April, they went to the Trust Bank building where the van was parked, unguarded, and poured two gallons of oil into the petrol tank. They followed the van the next day, but the oil apparently had no effect. That night they returned to the Trust Bank building. This time they added water to the fuel.

'The following day we followed the van,' Whitehead explained. 'It broke down as a result of the water and it was taken to a local garage for repair.'

At first they tried to get imprints of the keys, but were not successful. Van der Merwe then managed to steal the keys, which were kept in the van at the garage, have copies made, and return the originals with no-one any the wiser.

It was at this advanced stage of the operation that Whitehead decided to tell his wife of their plans, as they needed a third vehicle in case the security van was intercepted.

'I suspected something was in the air when Derek told me not to worry because they had a plan to get some money,' Jeanette Whitehead admitted, 'but I never expected it was going to be unlawful.'

A blazing row followed, but Whitehead was determined to go through with the plan. In the end, his wife agreed to drive their car – a fawn Mercedes – behind the security company's van. Her job was to remain nearby throughout the operation in case the two men required a getaway car.

Van der Merwe and Whitehead had false number plates made for the Mercedes and hired a Volkswagen kombi from a local garage. The kombi was to transport the money transferred from the security van.

On Tuesday, 27 April, 1971, they set out early in the morning to carry out the robbery. Derek Whitehead drove the kombi, while Jeanette Whitehead and Van der Merwe followed in the Mercedes. On this occasion, however, the security personnel only stayed inside the bank a few moments and the plan had to be aborted. They tried again the next day. At the second attempt, the whole operation went off as smooth as clockwork: Van der Merwe stepped out of the Mercedes, strolled over to the security van, let himself in and drove off.

On a patch of open ground a few blocks away from the bank, the money was swiftly transferred to the kombi. Mr A. Smith, an alert employee at an adjacent warehouse, witnessed the whole scene.

'I immediately became suspicious when I saw a red kombi and a fawn-coloured Mercedes driving around the security van,' Mr Smith said. 'And I managed to get a good look at the woman who was driving the Mercedes. She was a white woman in a red pill-box hat.'

After abandoning the security truck, the three robbers drove to Parktown, where they loaded the money into Van der Merwe's car and abandoned the kombi in the northern suburbs. Later that evening, they dumped the money boxes in the Vaal River near Vanderbijlpark. Whitehead packed the money into a space above the ceiling of his caravan and set off for Knysna with his wife and four children. They arrived in Knysna on Saturday, 1 May, and booked into the Brenton Hotel. Three days later, they were joined by Van der Merwe and his wife, Marlene. The couples immediately split up again. The Whiteheads moved to Brenton-on-Lake holiday resort, and the Van der Merwe's booked in at the Leisure Isle Hotel. On Sunday, 9 May, Tony and Marlene van der Merwe headed for Bloemfontein to visit Marlene's parents.

At the time of the robbery, the police had little or nothing to go on. Furthermore, the raid had been carried out with so much speed and precision, that they believed they were dealing with a team of professional bankrobbers. The fact that the robbers had been able to drive the van away with a set of duplicate keys was seen as highly significant and indicated an 'inside job'. However, the more they questioned the employees of the security firm, the more the police became convinced that they were not involved.

The police then broadened the scale of their enquiries to encompass anyone who was even remotely connected to the crime. They soon realised that duplicate keys had been obtained while the van was at the garage. Slowly, a picture emerged. After almost two weeks of intensive investigation, a tenuous link connected Van der Merwe to the crime and the police wanted to question him. However, when they called at his house, they found it locked. Neighbours believed he had gone to Bloemfontein with his wife to visit his in-laws.

By this time the police had established that Van der Merwe and Whitehead were in serious financial difficulties; that Van der Merwe resembled the man seen driving the security van; and that his Mercedes was similar to the one used in the robbery. Mr Smith had seen a fawn Mercedes when the money was transferred. On 10 May, the Brixton Murder and Robbery Squad asked the Orange Free State police to be on the lookout for Whitehead's Mercedes.

On Thursday, 13 May, Van der Merwe was spotted at a Bloemfontein roadblock. He was tailed to the house where he was staying and later arrested. Shortly afterwards, he made a full confession.

That evening, a police van with a police dog and handler from Knysna quietly drew up next to the Whitehead's caravan and spent the night on guard.

The Whitehead's were arrested at 3 a.m. on Friday morning at the Little Switzerland Hotel in the Drakensburg where they were staying.

They had arrived at 4.30 p.m. the previous day. A team of CID detectives from Johannesburg, the Orange Free State and Natal were involved in the swoop. After the arrest, the Whiteheads were taken to Bloemfontein for questioning and Jeanette Whitehead was taken to Johannesburg where she appeared briefly in court. A team of twelve detectives was flown back to the caravan park in two army helicopters.

That same Friday afternoon, Derek Whitehead and Willem Antonie van der Merwe were driven back to Knysna in a police car. Together, they unlocked the caravan and showed the detectives where the money was hidden. Sackfulls of money, mostly R10 notes, were removed from the ceiling of the caravan and stacked in the boot of the police car. Of the R240 000 stolen, all but R1 538 was recovered.

Derek Whitehead and Willem van der Merwe were remanded in custody pending trial. Jeanette Whitehead was granted bail of R1 000.

The trial of the Trust Bank robbers opened at the Rand Criminal Sessions on 14 June, 1971. All three accused pleaded guilty to the theft of R241 000 from the Trust Bank on 28 April, 1971.

After a two-day trial, the judge, Mr Justice M.E. Theron, delivered his verdict. He first postponed the passing of sentence on Jeanette Whitehead for three years, out of consideration for her children, and she was released.

'No doubt my leniency in this regard will be criticised,' he said, 'but I am prepared to face such critics. My tender feeling for her young children have persuaded me to deal with Mrs Whitehead as leniently as possible.' The judge also added that he accepted that Mrs Whitehead had 'passionately pleaded' with her husband to give up the scheme, 'fearing for his safety'.

A deeply distressed Mrs Whitehead was then taken from the court by an official.

Mr Justice Theron turned his attention to the two men. They stood condemned, he maintained, for the 'cold, calculated and ingenious way they had set about a scheme which might have been successful'.

He also pointed out that Whitehead and Van der Merwe had not acted on the impulse of sudden temptation, but had carefully planned the whole operation in detail. The fact that they were in a poor financial state was no excuse.

'It is my duty,' Mr Justice Theron concluded, 'to impose a severe sentence because the likelihood of hauls from financial institutions is a temptation and an evil which has to be stamped out.'

Hushed exclamations rose from the capacity crowd when he sentenced each of the two men to fourteen years in prison.

Gilbert Mthembu was arrested by the police following Van der Merwe's and Whitehead's full confession relating to the robbery and the events which led up to it.

In September 1971, the Appellate Division upheld the appeal of Whitehead and Van der Merwe against the severity of their sentences. The sentences for both men were reduced to 10 years.

In September 1971, Van der Merwe, Whitehead and Gilbert Mthembu appeared at Graaff-Reinet Regional Court in connection with their attempted robberies of Volkskas Banks at Uniondale and Aberdeen. The two men received additional one-year jail sentences.

Derek Whitehead and Willem Antonie van der Merwe were released on parole on 14 June, 1975, after serving only four years of their jail sentences.

18.

THE 'SCISSORS MURDER'

(MARLENE LEHNBERG: 1974)

On 4 November, 1974, Mrs Susanna Magdalena van der Linde, a forty-six year-old mother of three, was stabbed to death with a pair of scissors at her home in Gladstone Street, Boston Estate, Bellville. Her murderers were Marlene Lehnberg, (19), and a thirty-three year-old 'hired killer', Marthinus Choegoe.

Lehnberg's road to infamy began two-and-a-half years earlier in February 1972, when she began her first job as a clerical assistant/receptionist at the Red Cross Children's Hospital in Rondebosch. She started work in the orthopaedic workshop alongside the 'father figure' who was later to become her lover, Christiaan van der Linde (47). Van der Linde was the workshop's chief technician and Lehnberg, a bright, intelligent and attractive sixteen year-old, was drawn to him from the start.

'He struck me as something special,' she later admitted. 'He impressed me tremendously. "Welcome" he said and my heart beat faster.'

Lehnberg's upbringing had been both conservative and strict. Her father was puritanical, a man who rarely displayed any affection towards his daughter. It was not surprising, therefore, that she should be so drawn to Van der Linde, a person whom she saw as being warm and friendly.

Van der Linde said that he originally had a 'fatherly relationship' with Lehnberg, but they grew closer and closer as the months passed. Eventually, he found her impossible to resist. 'A determined, intelligent woman in love is difficult to contain,' Van der Linde said. In April 1973, barely a year after they first met, the couple began a tempestuous love affair that was ultimately to end in disaster.

Throughout the remainder of 1973, Lehnberg and Van der Linde continued to meet in secret – at Rondebosch common, Paarden Eiland and 'places like that'. Then, early in 1974, their intimacy stopped. People were watching them, Van der Linde said, and his wife was receiving anonymous telephone calls.

Despite the fact that Van der Linde had declared that he would never leave his wife and family, Lehnberg was convinced that the only obstacle to them having a more permanent relationship was the presence of Van der Linde's wife, Susanna.

By July 1974, Lehnberg was becoming desperate and started talking about leaving Cape Town. Christiaan van der Linde persuaded her not to, but by September she had finally tired of the situation and decided to bring matters to a head herself by speaking to his wife. She called her and explained that she and Christiaan were very much in love and were seeing each other every night. She wanted to know what Mrs van der Linde intended doing, but Mrs van der Linde put the telephone down on her. A few weeks later, Lehnberg telephoned again. This time she made an appointment to go and see her. They met in Bellville early in October.

Initially, Lehnberg had hoped that she and Mrs van der Linde could come to some sort of arrangement concerning Christiaan, but this meeting was to change all of those ideas. Not only did Mrs van der Linde tell Lehnberg that she would never give her husband a divorce because of the children, she also added a barb: 'I don't mind playing second fiddle,' she said, 'as long as you don't mind doing likewise.'

It was suddenly obvious to Lehnberg that Susanna van der Linde was prepared to do anything to keep her husband. It was equally obvious that she had only one alternative left – murder.

It was around this time that Marthinus Charles Choegoe (33) a miserable, scruffy-looking, unemployed cripple entered the scene. Choegoe, who had lost a leg in a motor-car accident, had come to the Orthopaedic Workshop to have an artificial limb fitted. His disabilities – both physical and social – had destroyed his self-esteem and this made him particularly susceptible to Lehnberg's approaches. In the end, he would become totally subservient to '*Miss* Lehnberg'.

Lehnberg first contacted Choegoe by letter, which she wrote to him care of Solly's Trading Store, his local shop. In the letter, she asked him to come and see her at the Orthopaedic Workshop and added, 'Marthinus, if you are clever you can still earn good money'. When he turned up at the workshop, Lehnberg gave him R1 and asked him to meet her at the Rondebosch town hall at 7 p.m..

Later that same evening, she gave him a bottle of gin and said that she wanted him to murder a woman for her.

'But Miss Marlene,' Choegoe replied, 'I can't do a thing like that. It will send me to the gallows.'

'Were you ever involved in a court case, Marthinus?' Lehnberg asked.

'Yes, I was charged with carrying a dangerous weapon.'

'Good,' she replied, 'because that's the sort of person I'm looking for. Someone who can handle a dangerous weapon.'

After some discussion, Choegoe finally agreed to Lehnberg's request. A couple of days later, he went to the address in Boston Estate which Lehnberg had given him.

'My plan was to warn her (Mrs van der Linde) that her life was in danger,' Choegoe claimed. When he got to Gladstone Street, however, instead of warning Mrs van der Linde of Lehnberg's plans, he asked her for some change. She said she hadn't got any and went back inside the house.

A week later, Choegoe and Lehnberg met in Rondebosch once more. This time he admitted that he was too afraid to go through with the murder. Lehnberg said that they 'would make his leg better at the hospital' if he 'did away' with Mrs van der Linde. She also gave him a radio. Choegoe went to Bellville once more. On this occasion, he simply walked past the house but made no attempt to enter.

Photograph courtesy of *The Argus*

Marlene Lehnberg

Shortly afterwards Lehnberg sent Choegoe a second letter. Again she urged him to go through with the murder. 'Use a knife if you have to,' she wrote, 'but make sure the job is done.' Then, she got another message to him, asking him to telephone her at work. During the subsequent conversation, Lehnberg insisted that Choegoe go through with the murder. She promised him a car and to have sex with him once the crime had been committed.

In October 1974, Lehnberg handed in her notice at the hospital and she told Christiaan van der Linde that she was going to leave Cape Town.

On 24 October, Lehnberg collected Choegoe from his home in Retreat and took him through to Bellville in her car. He was armed with a hammer, which was to be used to kill Mrs van der Linde. Lehnberg dropped him off in the vicinity of

Boston Estate and sped away. Shortly afterwards, Choegoe was spotted by Mrs van der Linde. She was alarmed, because she had seen him in the area on more than one occasion, and telephoned the Bellville Police Station. Choegoe was picked up by the police about two blocks from her house. At the police station he was beaten and warned not to return to the area.

In the face of repeated failure, Lehnberg decided to take matters into her own hands again.

A few days after Choegoe's failed attempt, she approached Rob Newman (24), an engineering student whom she knew, and asked to borrow his Llama pistol. When he refused, she asked if he would kill someone for her. Again, he refused. On 28 October, Newman's pistol was stolen from his room. He reported the theft to the police and suggested Lehnberg as a likely suspect.

Around 8.30 a.m. on the morning of Monday, 4 November, 1974, Lehnberg arrived at Choegoe's home. She said that her car was packed and she was on her way to Johannesburg, but before she left she needed Choegoe to come with her to Van der Linde's house. He claimed in a statement that it wasn't until she handed him the Llama pistol on the way to Bellville that he realized that she wasn't just going to say goodbye.

They arrived outside the house just after 9 a.m. Mrs van der Linde was alone inside. From this point on, Choegoe's account and Lehnberg's account of what followed, differ. Lehnberg claimed that she got out of the car, rang the doorbell and returned to the car while Choegoe entered the house alone and committed the murder. Choegoe, however, maintained that they acted in concert throughout. (Choegoe's account was supported by a neighbour of the Van der Linde's – Mrs Marais. On the morning in question, Mrs Marais had walked passed Lehnberg's white Ford Anglia twice in the space of ten or twelve minutes while it was parked opposite the Van der Linde house. On both occasions the car was empty.)

Choegoe said that after Lehnberg rang the bell, they went into the house together. When Mrs van der Linde saw them both, she became extremely frightened and threatened to telephone the police. She attempted to get away, but was tripped by Lehnberg, fell and hit her head on the door. While Mrs van der Linde was on the floor, Lehnberg struck her on the jaw with the pistol butt. On Lehnberg's instructions, Choegoe began to throttle the semi-conscious Mrs van der Linde. Lehnberg then gave him a pair of scissors she had taken from the sideboard.

'I remember stabbing her three times,' Choegoe said. (The pathologist noted seven stab wounds, six of which had penetrated the chest.)

After the murder, Lehnberg squirted green dye over Choegoe using a Wepron gas pistol belonging to Mrs van der Linde. (Mrs van der Linde kept the gas pistol, which was designed to deter intruders, behind a picture in the living room.) After warning Choegoe that she would deny any involvement in the murder if he went to the police, Lehnberg took him home. She set off for Johannesburg, collecting two speeding tickets at Beaufort West on the journey.

Choegoe kept both of the pistols that were used at the scene of the crime. They were later seized by the police. When Choegoe was asked why he hadn't thrown the pistols away, he replied: 'It is very dangerous to just throw pistols away.'

Susanna van der Linde's body was discovered at about 1 p.m..

Christiaan van der Linde attempted to telephone his wife a number of times that morning and eventually became concerned when there was no reply. He spoke to his daughter Zelda, who worked at Tygerberg Hospital, and asked her to go home during her lunch break to see if there was anything wrong.

When Miss van der Linde arrived home, the house was locked up, but through a window she caught a glimpse of her mother, who was lying on the floor in the living room and summoned the police.

The police immediately began an intensive murder investigation. Their chief suspect was 'a crippled Coloured man' who had been seen in the district on at least two occasions prior to the murder. (In fact, it was because of Choegoe that Mrs van der Linde insisted that her husband buy her a dye pistol.)

At first no-one considered that Lehnberg was involved, or that she could have hired an assassin.

For the next week, police efforts to establish Choegoe's identity and whereabouts proved fruitless. Then, on 13 November, the breakthrough occurred. At around 7.30 a.m. on the morning of 13 November, Lieutenant Roland Fourie of the Brixton Murder and Robbery Squad went to see Lehnberg, who was staying at her uncle's house in Bryanston, and asked her to accompany him to Brixton Police Station where he wished to ask her some questions. Lehnberg admitted on the way to the police station that Christiaan van der Linde was her lover and that she had been expecting the police to contact her in connection with the death of his wife ever since she had learnt of the murder of Susanna van der Linde from her mother.

When asked if she had an association with 'a Coloured man named Marthinus' she denied the allegation. Lieutenant Fourie also asked her if she had once requested a Mr Robert Newman to give her his pistol so that she could 'get rid of her' (Mrs van der Linde). Lehnberg admitted that she had, but that the request had been made in fun.

Although Lieutenant Fourie had no specific evidence to tie Lehnberg to the murder, it did strike him that she seemed unnaturally nervous at times during the interview.

While Lieutenant Fourie was on the telephone to Cape Town, another detective, Major van Aswegen, began asking Lehnberg questions. Suddenly, she blurted out, 'I took the guy there. I waited for him. He came back and I took him home.'

Lehnberg was arrested and formally charged with the murder of Mrs van der Linde. Later that day, she made a full statement in which she admitted that she had asked Marthinus [Choegoe], a leg patient at the Red Cross Hospital, if he would 'do away' with Mrs van der Linde. In the statement she claimed that she had waited in the car while her accomplice had committed the crime. Choegoe was arrested the same day.

The trial of Marlene Lehnberg and Marthinus Charles Choegoe began at the Cape Town Supreme Court on 5 March, 1975.

The trial drew hundreds of spectators who fought for seats in the packed courtroom.

After a hearing which lasted seven days and during which the State called more than 30 witnesses, the Judge, Mr Justice Diemont, and his two assessors, Mr A.J. van Niekerk and Mr F. van Zyl Smith, deliberated overnight after which they returned verdicts of guilty for both accused. The court found no extenuating circumtances and Lehnberg and Choegoe were sentenced to death.

'I have presided over many cases but have never heard evidence as strange and bizarre as this one,' Mr Justice Diemont admitted.

Two months later, the case was re-opened on appeal. In July 1975, the death sentences were set aside. Lehnberg was sentenced to 20 years imprisonment and Choegoe to 15 years.

Choegoe, however, was released in June 1986 and became an evangelical preacher, while Lehnberg was paroled in December of the same year.

The third member of the tragic triangle, Christiaan van der Linde, died a lonely man in 1983. After the trial, he moved to Krugersdorp so that he could visit his wife's grave on her family's farm in the Magaliesberg 'almost every day'.

'My dear wife is dead,' he once told a reporter. 'I sincerely wish to God that I had never set eyes on Marlene Lehnberg.'

19.

THE INFORMATION SCANDAL

(1979–80)

In the latter part of the 1970s, South Africa was rocked by a major political scandal involving the Department of Information, which was allegedly misappropriating State funds for secret projects. The Information Scandal (or *Infogate* or *Rhoodiegate* or *Muldergate*), as it came to be known, was to culminate in the resignation of Cabinet Minister Dr Connie Mulder and the State President, B.J. Vorster.

One of the main players in this colourful drama was Eschel Rhoodie and his story really begins in Pretoria eight years earlier.

At the beginning of 1971, Eschel Rhoodie, then Press Officer of the South African embassy at The Hague, clandestinely negotiated an agreement with a Dutch publisher by the name of Hubert Jussen whereby Jussen agreed to help with the establishment of a new magazine – *To the Point*. *To the Point* was to be secretly financed by the South African government and was intended to counter some of the unfavourable press coverage South Africa was receiving overseas. This secret scheme had the approval the Prime Minister, B.J. Vorster; the chief of the Intelligence Services, General Hendrik van den Bergh; the Minister of Information, Dr Connie Mulder; and Mr Gerald Barrie, the then head of the Department of Information. *To the Point* was launched before the end of the year.

In July 1972, Rhoodie was appointed to the post of Secretary of Information. He was young, dynamic, enterprising and impatient – particularly with the bureaucratic process. These were the qualities that enabled him to get things done. With the advantage of hindsight, one might say, these were the things which enabled him to get things done *too* well.

Shortly after his appointment to what would be called the 'Dirty Tricks' Department, Rhoodie recruited as his deputies Les de Villiers and his own brother, Deneys. Initially, *To the Point* was the only secret project in operation, but the Bureau of State Security had plans for a number of other schemes and a long list of 'spooks' (secret agents) willing to see them through.

It wasn't long before a second project was instituted. This time it was the creation of an organisation designed to counter South Africa's sporting isolation.

The result was the Committee for Fairness in Sport.

Then came a scheme involving a group of influential businessmen abroad. The 'Club of Ten', as the group was known, had the difficult task of tackling the media, the United Nations, other institutions, individuals and countries for their double-dealing and hypocrisy where South Africa was concerned. Not an easy task! A number of influential individuals operated more covertly to improve South Africa's image abroad.

From 1973 onwards, by which time Rhoodie was working in close co-operation with 'the power behind the throne' – General Hendrik van den Bergh, the head of BOSS – new schemes and projects were constantly being introduced. They were all run by Eschel Rhoodie's Department of Information and they were all paid for with government money. Due to the delicacy of the situation, money was often handed over in cash – without any receipt.

In February 1974, Prime Minister Vorster gave official approval to covert action at a meeting in Cape Town attended by Rhoodie, Mulder and the Finance Minister, Nico Diederichs. Since it had become evident that the conventional methods that governments used to express opinions – in the form of films, brochures and hand-outs – were no longer effective, Vorster accepted that it was necessary to wage an all-out psychological assault on foreign opinion. New rules and systems were to be applied. Only objectives would count and the end would justify the means – any means.

Towards the end of 1975, project Annemarie was conceived. (Annemarie was the name of Rhoodie's teenage daughter.) This was for the introduction of an English-language newspaper to counter attacks on the government by the English press – particularly the *Rand Daily Mail.* The man chosen to front this operation was Dr Louis Luyt, the fertilizer millionaire.

The first salvo in what was to become something of a newspaper war was when Luyt attempted to buy up shares of SAAN (South African Associated Newspapers). To give credibility to his take-over attempt, he went on television to explain his new-found interest in publishing. He also took the opportunity to announce that he had two prominent overseas publishers supporting his bid for SAAN. Despite Luyt's overtures to some of SAAN's major shareholders, his take-over attempt was blocked.

Luyt then announced that he intended to create his own independent newspaper, which would go on to the streets in the second half of 1976. The name he chose for this newspaper was the *Citizen*.

The cost of running the newspaper was estimated to be around R130 000 per month, but it was expected that the paper would pay for itself as time went on. At the *Rand Daily Mail,* the news that another English-medium newspaper was to arrive on the scene was greeted with disbelief. The *Rand Daily Mail* itself was losing money and was being supported by the mass circulation *Sunday Times*. Nevertheless, the *Rand Daily Mail* took Luyt seriously since he had never made empty threats. The owners of the *Rand Daily Mail* were also acutely aware that 25% of their readership had only a loose association with the newspaper and could be convinced to change. A struggle for survival was anticipated.

Photograph courtesy of *Die Burger*

Eschel and Katie Rhoodie

Meanwhile, a loan of R12-million was set aside to finance project Annemarie on the understanding that once the newspaper became financially self-supporting, this money would be returned to the State's coffers.

Unfortunately, the scheme was beset with problems. By the time the first edition of the newspaper was on the streets on 7 September, 1976, Luyt, Rhoodie and their associates had already been forced to surmount a number of crises. Even after the newspaper went into full production, matters didn't improve.

By March 1977, the situation had become serious. The *Citizen*'s growth was falling well short of expectations, and relations between Luyt and Rhoodie had deteriorated – almost to the stage of open hostility. But the worst was yet to come...

At the beginning of 1976, there had been general consensus in the government and the opposition that the Department of Information was doing a good job. Even then, however, trouble was brewing behind the scenes.

The money used by the Department of Information was obtained through the Department of Defence, since it was assumed that a few million rands would hardly be noticed in a budget that exceeded over R1-billion. Unfortunately, the defence account neglected to add the Department of Information money to the amount requisitioned from the Treasury. By the time the mistake was made apparent, there were no funds available. To make matters worse, the Minister of Defence, P.W. Botha, was unhappy about his department being used to finance a secret project.

The first rumblings of internal discontent and scandal were surfacing.

By July 1977, rumours and speculation concerning financial malpractice in the Department of Information became so serious that an audit of the department's books was ordered. There was also talk of the *Citizen* and the Department of Information being linked.

Towards the end of 1977, Luyt decided to withdraw from the newspaper. (The *Citizen* was formally transferred to its new publishers, Jussens and Van Zyl Alberts, in February 1978.)

In November 1977, Les de Villiers, one of Rhoodie's deputies, also resigned from the Department of Information, a job he had held for 17 years, and joined a public relations firm, Sidney Baron, in New York. Finally, in the face of mounting criticism, in May 1978, Dr Connie Mulder had to answer for his department in Parliament. In response to questions tabled in the House, he declared categorically that the *Citizen* was not financed by government money. (It was as a result of this lie that he would eventually be disgraced and disbarred.)

In the autumn of 1978, the Information Affair reached crisis proportions. The Minister of Finance, Owen Horwood, instituted an inquiry under the auspices of Judge Anton Mostert to probe exchange-control violations. On 2 November, 1978, despite protestations from the new Prime Minister, P.W. Botha, and Minister Horwood, Justice Mostert called a press conference to divulge details of the 'scandal'.

On Wednesday, 3 November, under the heading *It's all True* the *Rand Daily Mail* wrote:

> South Africa's biggest bombshell burst yesterday when Mr Justice Anton Mostert made public startling evidence which has confirmed reports in the *Rand Daily Mail* and *Sunday Express* of massive misuse of public money through Department of Information secret funds. Judge Mostert released evidence which shows beyond doubt that the *Citizen* newspaper was financed through State funds. And in evidence under oath, Mr Louis Luyt named the former Prime Minister, Mr Vorster, the Minister of Plural Relations, Dr Connie Mulder and General Hendrik van den Bergh, former head of the Bureau of State Security, as key figures in the secret project to finance the newspaper.

In the same month, Prime Minister Botha instituted a judicial commission of inquiry into the whole affair under the chair of Mr Justice Roelof Erasmus. Eschel

Rhoodie, who had already had his passport withdrawn, was summoned before the commission, gave testimony, then vanished.

Mulder, meanwhile, was being vilified by the media. He was first stripped of his Cabinet post, then his leadership of the National Party in the Transvaal, and was finally forced to resign his parliamentary seat. In a similar fashion, State President Vorster also resigned his presidency under a cloud of suspicion after being severely censured by the Erasmus Commission. In the commission's interim report, Rhoodie was accused of misappropriating State funds.

P.W. Botha and a number of other prominent government figures, were completely exonerated with regard to any involvement in the secret projects of the information scandal. (The final report of the Erasmus Commission was published in June 1979.)

Although in the eyes of the public the *Citizen* newspaper was largely discredited, Johnny Johnson, the then editor vehemently denied the accusation that the paper was little more than a National Party organ. In an editorial on 6 December, 1978 he wrote:

> The *Citizen* was started and funded with Government money. That is the finding of the Erasmus Commission. But the Government did not direct the *Citizen's* editorial policy. That is the assurance I have already given as editor-in-chief of this publication. And it is an assurance which I repeat today, when the newspaper is at the centre of a new storm of controvesy. The *Citizen* – and I cannot emphasise this strongly enough – was not, and is not, a government propaganda medium of the National Party.

In February 1979, journalists finally tracked Rhoodie to ground in Ecuador. By this time he was South Africa's *Most Wanted Man* and the government had instituted legal proceedings against him. In March 1979, Rhoodie moved to Great Britain where he attempted, albeit unsuccessfully, to gain political asylum. In a BBC television interview with David Dimbleby on March 21, 1979, he strongly denied the accusations made against him, reiterating his claim that he was being made a scapegoat for the whole affair, and maintained that senior government figures, including the then Prime Minister, P.W. Botha, were both aware of and sanctioned the secret projects he had conducted as head of the Department of Information.

Shortly afterwards, Rhoodie moved to France, where he was eventually arrested by the French authorities and incarcerated for 88 days pending extradition to South Africa.

The trial of Dr Eschel Rhoodie began at the Pretoria Supreme Court on 22 September, 1979. He was charged with seven counts of fraud, alternatively theft, involving a total of R63 205 of government money.

Despite the fact that it was shown during the trial that he controlled a series of slush funds in Switzerland, Holland and Britain to finance the Information Department's secret projects – a total of between R18- and R20-million, of which 'not a cent was missing' – he was found guilty on 8 October of five charges of fraud and sentenced to an effective six years' imprisonment. On 9 October he was granted bail of R90 000 pending an appeal.

A year later, in October 1980, Dr Eschel Rhoodie was acquitted on all counts involving State monies by the Appeal Court in Bloemfontein. The following day, he gave a press conference and issued a ten-page statement in which he expressed his abhorrence and outrage at the treatment he had received at the hands of the South African government. Amongst other things, he declared:

'I have always maintained I was innocent and that the case against me was a political one. That is why I strenuously resisted the government's efforts to extradite me from France. It was a handful of powerful politicians who used the apparatus of the State, not to mention a vast sum of taxpayers' money, to destroy me and my family, socially, politically and financially. There were other victims too, outside my family, but they must speak for themselves. These politicians launched a vendetta against the Rhoodie family in 1978, in an all-out effort to crush us, primarily to protect their own involvement in the government's secret propaganda war of 1971 to 1978.

'I reject totally the Erasmus Commission's whitewash of those ministers.'

It was estimated that the South African government spent R500 000 to establish that Dr Eschel Rhoodie was innocent of the fraud charges brought against him.

In March 1982, Dr Eschel Rhoodie and his wife Katie emigrated to the United States. His book *The Real Information Scandal*, which was published in October 1983, contained sweeping allegations of big-name involvement in secret 'Info' projects. He further maintained that dozens of senior government officials were aware of the secret projects his department actively pursued, and that R75-million had been allocated over a five-year period to finance these projects. Official figures released when the scandal broke accounted for only R64-million.

Dr Rhoodie and his wife still reside in the United States, where he continues to write and pursue his business interests.

His most recent book: *P.W. Botha: The Last Betrayal 1978-1989*, was published in 1990.

20. THE STANDER GANG (1983–84)

Between October 1983, and February 1984, the Stander Gang, comprising Andre Charles Stander (37), Patrick Lee McCall (34) and Allan Heyl (32), were South Africa's *Most Wanted Men*.

Their story is one of daring prison escapes, dramatic bank robberies and – inevitably – violent death. In other words, the stuff of legend. It is not surprising, therefore, that for some people Stander, McCall and Heyl have become something akin to folk heroes.

In reality, they were simply three hardened criminals on a desperate flight from justice.

Andre Stander, the mastermind and driving force behind the Stander Gang, was the son of Major-General Frans Stander. As a police detective, and later a bank-robber, he was sometimes described as 'brilliant' although he was a less-than-average student at school. He failed his matric and was pressurized by his father into joining the police force. Nevertheless, he excelled at Police College and was judged 'Best Recruit' in 1964. After graduating from Police College in Pretoria, Stander joined the regular force and was sent to Johannesburg. He rose rapidly through the ranks, and by the age of thirty-one held the rank of captain and was head of the Kempton Park Criminal Investigation Department.

Despite a blossoming career in the police force, Stander was obviously a discontented man. To compensate for whatever was missing in his life, he took to robbing banks as a sideline. This started in 1977. On his days off, he would catch an early-morning flight to Durban, where he would don a disguise, hire or steal a car, and then set out for his target. At the bank or building society in question, he would hold up the teller at gunpoint, take the money, and then casually drive back to the airport. It was all very simple and professional.

During the three years that Stander operated alone, he hit a string of banks and netted himself at least R100 000. In fact, he became so successful he couldn't keep his mouth shut and approached his best friend, Cor van Deventer, who was then working for the Bureau of State Security, and invited him to join the fun.

'He admitted to me that the first few times were sheer agony,' Van Deventer said. 'But after that he couldn't stop. He began to enjoy himself. He used to watch the faces of his victims. He was laughing up his sleeve when he committed his robberies. There was an element of sadistic bullying...'

Eventually, Van Deventer approached a senior colleague and told him what his friend had said. Together, the two men went to examine a hired car which Stander claimed to have stolen and parked at Jan Smuts airport. In the glove compartment they found a balaclava, a number of wigs, and a false beard and moustache. In the boot there was a false number plate and a roll of masking tape. They returned the items to the car and then staked it out. On 2 January, 1980, Stander was observed removing a number of items from the car. The following day, a bank was robbed in Durban.

On 4 January, Stander flew into Johannesburg from Durban. In the presence of Major-General Kobus Visser, the commander of the CID, he was arrested in the arrivals lounge and escorted to the car. He had R4 000 on him, a balaclava, a revolver, and a false moustache and beard in his luggage.

Following his arrest, Stander was remanded in custody. On 6 May, 1980, he faced 28 charges of robbery at the Durban Supreme Court. He was found guilty on 15 charges and sentenced to a total of 75 years in prison. As some of the sentences were to run concurrently, he faced an effective jail term of 17 years.

'I forced him to become a policeman against his wishes,' his father admitted after the trial. 'He should have left the force years ago.'

No one has been able to explain why Stander turned so suddenly to crime. His family claimed that his behaviour was in response to his experiences during the township unrest in Tembisa in 1976, when he was involved in a 'bloodbath', but Cor van Deventer disputes this.

'I don't accept that,' he said. 'He was supposed to have shot 22 people, but I never heard about it. Don't you think he would have told his best friend about it at some time or other? If it had really happened...'

Part of the reason may have been that Stander's marriage was also under strain during this time. He had first met his wife, Leonie, in 1967. They were married in 1969, and divorced two years later. In 1975 they remarried, but Leonie walked out on him in 1978. They were divorced for a second time in 1979.

The most likely answer is that Stander simply enjoyed the thrill of robbing banks, which may partly explain the myth that built up around his name. And myth indeed it was.

During the height of the search for the Stander Gang, an ex-colleague of Stander's, Chris Swanepoel, remarked to the press, 'You know we read every day of the brilliant student who was forced on the road to robbery. Brilliant? How could he be brilliant and still fail matric? Sure he was a captain of the police but was he a brilliant detective? Rubbish, I say! When we were in the force together he couldn't even catch a cold...

He was seen by many people as a 'gentleman robber', a kind of modern-day Robin Hood, but the police also alleged that he was a rapist. In October 1983, while he was on the run from the police, Stander lured a teenage girl to the Kyalami Ranch Hotel for a photographic session. She was to pose fully clothed and he claimed to be a reputable photographer. After the session, he raped her and then threatened to cut her to pieces if she told anyone about what had happened. It was only later that she discovered Stander's identity. Photographs of the girl were also discovered at one of the Stander Gang's hideouts. There is also evidence that Stander raped another teenage girl in a similar fashion.

After his conviction for armed robbery, Stander was sent to Zonderwater maximum security prison near Cullinan. It was here that he met Patrick Lee McCall and Allan Heyl. Both men were bank robbers, and McCall was also an expert car thief.

On 11 August, 1983, Stander, McCall and five other prisoners were taken out of the prison to see a local physiotherapist at consulting rooms near Cullinan. Stander and McCall had faked their injuries. The seven prisoners were accompanied by three prison officers.

In the waiting room, Stander and McCall suddenly sprang into action, overpowered the guards and took their service revolvers. They then ordered Mrs Amelia Grobler, the physiotherapist, to give them the keys to her car. They sped off in the direction of Tembisa township. The other five prisoners, who had refused to have anything to do with the breakout, remained behind.

About seven kilometres from Cullinan, Stander and McCall turned on to a dirt road. They eventually arrived at a farm belonging to Mr Martin Riekert in the Rayton district. They were greeted in the yard by Mr Riekert and his teenage son, Henk. At gunpoint they forced Mr Riekert to telephone the local police station on a pretence, whereupon Police Constable Mostert was sent to the farm. Stander and McCall were waiting for him. He was first forced to change clothes with Stander, and was then bundled into the back of his own van along with Mr Riekert and his son. With the three hostages locked in the cage of the police van, Stander and McCall continued in the direction of Tembisa township.

On a secluded road not far from the farm, they stopped again. Stander got out of the van and flagged down the next car that came along – a silver-grey Opel driven by a 27-year-old nurse named Nakkie Fouche. Ms Fouche was bundled into the back of the police van along with the other three hostages. Stander and McCall then drove off in her car. The prisoners eventually escaped from the police van by kicking out the window between the cage and the cab, but by that time the two fugitives were long gone.

After escaping from custody, Stander and McCall went to ground for a while. For two months they lived quietly in Johannesburg on money it is thought Stander had stashed away during his bank-robbing days. However, on 31 October, 1983, the two men hit the news headlines again. At 10.30 a.m., they burst into the Olifantsfontein Trade Test Centre with guns drawn and released Allan Heyl, who had been taken there for a trade test. After forcing the two prison warders who were guarding Heyl and the three members of the Trade Centre staff to lie on the floor, they sped off in a Ford Cortina XR6 Interceptor. For the next four months, the Stander Gang, as the trio came to be known, were to be front page news.

Ten days later, Stander, McCall and Heyl raided a gunshop in Randburg, wounding the proprietor in the process, and made off with an arsenal of heavy-calibre guns and ammunition. Then, operating from at least three 'safe houses' in the Johannesburg area, the three men went on a spree of 'bank-hopping' robberies in which they hit a string of banks in quick succession, sometimes as many as four on the same day. Between mid-November 1983, and mid-January 1984, the Stander Gang robbed twenty banks and stole over R500 000. On 19 January, alone, they netted R165 000 from three jobs!

Nevertheless, the three men realised that time was running out for them. Indeed, Stander himself had come close to arrest more than once. On one occasion he had been in a video shop in Turffontein when it was raided by the police, but had not been recognized. On another occasion, he had been spotted by a police captain at a Maseru restaurant but had managed to get away.

The answer was to go abroad and to this end the three men planned to buy a yacht which they could sail out of the country. Towards the end of 1983, they saw just the vessel they were looking for at the Royal Cape Yacht Club in Cape Town. She was the *Lily Rose* and the asking price was R219 000. In January 1984, negotiations to purchase the *Lily Rose* began in earnest.

It was also in January that the police received an important break when Stander, McCall and Heyl were photographed by hidden video cameras during a bank robbery. For the first time since the men had broken out of prison, the police had good recent photographs of them. Pictures of the three wanted men were published on 25 January.

On 27 January, Stander flew to Fort Lauderdale in the USA using a false passport. His task was to arrange the sale of the *Lily Rose*.

Back in South Africa, a tip-off following the publication of the Stander Gang photographs led the police to one of the 'safe houses' in Sixth Avenue, Houghton.

Much assistance in identifying the safe houses reputedly came from escort girls who had been employed by members of the gang and taken to their hideouts. On the day after Stander left the country, the place was staked out and in the early hours of 30 January, 1984, a crack police squad moved into position with marksmen in bullet-proof vests taking up strategic positions. At 5 a.m. the silence in the neighbourhood was shattered by a loud-hailer. The message from the police was clear and simple: 'Get out of the house or we shoot.'

McCall was alone inside, and he was determined to go down fighting rather than surrender. Darting from room to room, he began to shoot at his attackers. A tremendous gun battle followed, with the police eventually hurling grenades into the house and storming in. They found McCall sprawled naked in the hall. He was dead.

Twenty-four hours later, the police discovered a second 'safe house' at Linmeyer due to the publicity that the gang was receiving. They also learnt of the scheme to buy the *Lily Rose* from a crew member that Stander and Heyl hired to deliver the yacht to the USA. On 5 February, the police flew to Cape Town and seized the R219 000 boat.

A few days later, the police discovered a third hideout, again in Houghton, which had been hired on a one-year lease at R2 000 per month. In the garage were a number of stolen cars, including a yellow Porsch Targa which Stander himself was known to like. But of Stander and Heyl nothing was known. Both men had flown the coop.

Stander was in America, and ten days after McCall had been killed, he made his own fatal mistake.

On 10 February, Stander was arrested by the Fort Lauderdale police for driving an unlicensed vehicle – a Ford Mustang which he had recently bought from a second-hand car dealer named Anthony Tomasello – and for forging a driver's licence. The car was impounded by the police and Stander, who claimed to be an Australian author named Peter Harris, was photographed and released. That same night, he broke into the police pound and stole the car back again. The next morning, he took it back to Tomasello and asked him to have it resprayed.

Unfortunately for Stander, that very morning Tomasello had been reading about the exploits of the Stander Gang in his local newspaper, the *Sun Sentinel*, just as 'Peter Harris' walked into his office. He put two and two together. The moment Stander departed, Tomasello got in touch with his lawyer, who advised him to contact the police.

That night an élite tactical impact team surrounded Stander's apartment. At 10.30 p.m., Stander rode up on a bicycle. He was confronted by Officer

Michael von Stetina, but attempted to escape. There was a brief struggle for Stetina's shotgun and Stander was shot. He bled to death on the wet driveway to his apartment block while waiting for an ambulance.

After the death of Patrick Lee McCall, Allan Heyl left South Africa and moved to the picturesque Greek island of Hydra. From Hydra he flew to England, where he made a payroll snatch which netted a mere R4 000 – he had expected the haul to top R300 000 – then he moved to Spain. He was later forced to enlist the help of a confidence trickster named Billy Williams. Williams, who was supposed to help Heyl reclaim money and valuables left stashed in Britain, first took all he could for himself, then went to Scotland Yard and gave the police details of his new identity, Phillip John Ball, and his address in the United Kingdom. The British press would later label Williams 'Supergrass'.

Not long afterwards, Heyl was arrested at his girlfriend's mother's house in Surrey, England.

In May 1985, at Winchester Crown Court, Allan Heyl was sentenced to nine years in prison for armed robbery and illegal possession of a firearm.

Following Heyl's arrest, the South African authorities attempted to have him extradited to face charges in South Africa, despite the fact that no extradition treaty between Great Britain and South Africa existed.

For a time Heyl's fate hung in the balance. In December 1986, this 'very complicated' matter was finally resolved when the British Government announced that Heyl was to remain in Britain.

At the time of writing (January 1991) Allan Heyl is still in prison.

21.

SHE HIRED ASSASSINS TO MURDER HER HUSBAND

(LINDI MANGALISO: 1984)

On the night of 16 December, 1984, a wealthy Guguletu businessman, Victor Mangaliso, was stabbed to death in his luxurious Malunga Park home by two paid assassins, Sipo Peter (33) and Solomon Mbuzeli Shelini (43). At the time of his death, Mangaliso's life was insured for almost R500 000, and in the event of him being permanently disabled or paralysed, the value of his insurance policies increased to a staggering R1,2-million.

It would subsequently turn out that the two men who were involved in the killing were paid between R500 and R800 for carrying out the murder by Lindi Mangaliso, the victim's wife.

During the trial that followed, the Investigating Officer, Captain (now Major) Leonard Knipe, of the Peninsula Murder and Robbery Squad, would remark, 'Never in my experience as a policeman has there been a case which has gripped the imagination of the black community like this one.'

Lindi Nomsa Mangaliso (*nee* Qunta) was the eldest of five children. She came from a good home and had grown up surrounded by love. Her mother, who was a member of the Fingo tribe and related to the Dhlaminis, the Swazi royal family, held a Bachelor of Arts degree in Social Science. Her late father was a graduate of Fort Hare University and held both Bachelor of Arts and Bachelor of Education degrees. He had been the principal of Langa High School for more than twenty years and was highly respected in the community.

After matriculating from Langa High School, Lindi qualified as a nurse in Port Elizabeth. In 1972, while still a student nurse, she married Victor Mangaliso, who at the time worked in a bottle store. Initially, Mr and Mrs Qunta objected to the match – Victor's prospects were poor; his father worked as a cook in a hospital, and his mother was an unemployed domestic worker – but in the end, Lindi talked them round. After her marriage, she moved into a house with her in-laws in Guguletu.

After completing her training, Lindi obtained a nursing post at Groote Schuur Hospital. While still a nursing sister, she ventured into business for herself using her own capital and some money her mother had given her. She first bought a butchery in Langa, which was followed by a second one, and then she finally acquired the franchise for a Kentucky Fried Chicken outlet in Guguletu. Eventually, she decided to go into business full-time.

Her husband by this time was a representative for Nestlé but he later began to work for his wife. Lindi's mother maintained that Lindi was the one with the ideas and business acumen and that Victor was merely a glorified bookkeeper.

'As the business prospered,' she said, 'they bought a home in the name of his mother because they wanted something more prestigious. Later they bought their own home. They lived very well.'

Throughout the marriage, Mr and Mrs Qunta remained concerned about their daughter, whose strong personality aroused violent reactions in her husband. Victor took a sucession of girlfriends, drank heavily, and often became violent.

'Sometimes she would call me at 2 a.m. and ask me to fetch her,' Mrs Qunta said. 'I would ask my son to collect her. On occasions she had a black eye which she tried to hide with sunglasses. At other times Lindi would phone and say that Victor was assaulting her. I would ask my son to take me to her home. I would talk to Victor. I felt it was useless because he was drunk. When he was sober he was very nice and used to say, "Yes, Mama". It was very humiliating for Lindi and things did not improve over the years.'

After putting up with her husband's womanizing, drinking and assaults for twelve years, Lindi felt 'angry' and 'humiliated'. She had made a number of attempts to save the marriage, all to no avail, and her life had finally become a misery. In the latter half of 1984, she decided to murder her husband.

To this end, she turned for help to one of her employees, Washington 'Manyosi' Nxawe, who was working in one of her butcheries. Although Nxawe had only been in Mrs Mangaliso's employ for about two months, she confided in him. 'She told me that she no longer loved her husband as he was playing the fool with her,' Nxawe said. 'She asked me to get people to beat him up.'

At first Nxawe was sceptical, but after Mrs Mangaliso had spoken to him three times, he realised how serious she was. He also knew that she was prepared to pay 'plenty of money' to have her husband done away with. Eventually, Nxawe approached another man – Sipo Peter. One night, a month or so after Mrs Mangaliso first approached him, Nxawe arranged a meeting between Mrs Mangaliso, Peter and another man by the name of Mbuzeli Shelini. At the meeting, Mrs Mangaliso told the two men that she wanted them to attack her husband. That night, however, Victor returned home very late, by which time the two men had gone. 'My husband is a very lucky man,' Mrs Mangaliso afterwards remarked.

A little while later, Mrs Mangaliso asked Nxawe if Peter could be trusted.

'I told Lindi that Sipo could be trusted,' Nxawe said. 'He was a brave man and would not divulge secrets as he was not a talkative man.'

A few days before the murder, the Mangaliso marriage faced another crisis. Lindi discovered that her husband had yet another girlfriend – this time a schoolgirl – and confronted him with the fact. Victor resented the way she had treated the whole affair and after at first denying everything, he eventually owned up and apologised.

As far as Lindi was concerned, however, this was the final straw. On 15 December, she phoned Nxawe. 'Sipo and his friend must do the job,' she said. 'Beat him up, paralyse or kill him!'

The following night, at about 2 a.m., Victor was called out of the house to investigate a burglar alarm which had gone off for the second time that night in one of the butcheries. It turned out to be a false alarm, but this only seemed to worsen his mood. Angrily, he telephoned his wife.

'He said I had to get the hell out of the house when he got home,' she said.

Mrs Mangaliso thought that she was going to be beaten again when her husband got home. In a state close to panic she telephoned Nxawe.

'Victor has phoned me,' she said. 'Get those guys you said you would get.'

Nxawe promised to do so but didn't call back. Not long afterwards, Mrs Mangaliso phoned him again, wanting to know where the men were. Nxawe explained that he hadn't been able to get hold of them. 'Go and find them,' she ordered.

Shortly afterwards, Nxawe, Peter and Shelini drove up to the house. Nxawe hooted twice and Mrs Mangaliso came to the door and let Peter and Shelini into the house. Nxawe then drove off. One of the men carried a knife and Mrs Mangaliso gave one of her own knives to the other. She showed them the main bedroom, the bathroom and where about R2 000 was hidden before taking them to the childrens' room, where they hid.

Eventually, Victor got back to the house. 'I am not in the mood to beat you otherwise I would have beaten the daylights out of you,' he said. He made himself a snack and went to bed. After he had retired for the night the two men crept into the bedroom. Lindi was lying awake in the darkness, waiting for the two men to appear.

'The bedroom door opened after a while,' she said. 'I ran out of the room and was aware of two people entering the bedroom. I ran to the bathroom. I heard my husband saying, "What do you want?"'

'Where is the money?' one of the men replied.

Shortly afterwards, someone locked the bathroom door from the outside. She heard the sounds of a struggle and climbed through the bathroom window. After alerting the servants, she ran to a neighbour's house. It was hours later that she learnt her husband was dead.

At first the police suspected that the murder had been the work of an ANC hit-squad. (A few months earlier, attempts had been made to extort money from a number of prominent black leaders and death threats had been issued. At the time, Mrs Mangaliso had claimed that neither she nor her husband were 'interested in township or national politics'.)

As the police investigation continued, however, a number of anomalies revealed themselves. In her first statement, Mrs Mangaliso claimed that she had been asleep next to her husband when the intruders entered the bedroom, yet there was no blood on her nightclothes, nor could she explain why the robbers had attacked and so brutally murdered her husband, yet left her untouched. Furthermore, the account she gave of the way she escaped from the bathroom and raised the alarm did not stand up to close examination.

Eventually, the police arrested Nxawe, who was charged with conspiracy to commit murder. In exchange for immunity from prosecution, Nxawe later turned State's evidence and named his accomplices.

The trial of Lindi Mangaliso, Sipo Peter and Mbuzeli Shelini, all of whom were charged with murder, began at the Cape Town Supreme Court on 18 March, 1986. All three accused pleaded not guilty.

After a lengthy trial, which was delayed by a number of interruptions and the fact that two of the accused changed counsel, Mangaliso, Sipo and Shelini were found guilty of murder on 24 November, 1986. In his four-hour summing-up of the marathon trial, Mr Justice de Kock said that the total evidence showed that Mangaliso 'planned and arranged the attack on Mr Mangaliso with the assistance of Washington "Manyosi" Nxawe and admitted the assailants to the house intending them to attack and kill her husband,' and, 'at least stood by' while her husband was attacked.

The court also rejected the claim by Shelini that he was an innocent party in the affair in that he remained standing in the passage while Peter stabbed Mr Mangaliso. Referring to a letter (*see box*) allegedly written in Pollsmoor prison by Shelini, where he was remanded during the trial, Mr Justice de Kock said that it was clear from the contents that he admitted he took part in the crime 'and that he fears the consequences that will follow'.

The court also rejected Peter's evidence that he was ill in bed on the night of the killing. The court accepted as admissable evidence – despite the fact that he would later claim the statement was made under duress – Peter's earlier statement in which he admitted that he and Shelini were taken to the Mangaliso's house where they fought with and killed Mr Mangaliso.

Sentence was finally passed on 12 December, 1986. Peter and Shelini were condemned to hang because they had 'deliberately and willingly taken part in this heinous crime for financial gain'. Mrs Mangaliso was sentenced to 20 years in prison. Her husband's 'abuse, betrayal and humiliation' were seen as extenuating circumstances.

On occasion, Mrs Winnie Mandela, who was a bosom friend of Lindi Mangaliso, attended the trial. As she was leaving the court on 4 December, she was pelted with softdrink cans, orange peel and sand by a large, angry crowd. 'Winnie Mandela is the wife of our leader,' one protester maintained. 'She should not be supporting Lindi Mangaliso!'

Mrs Mandela later blamed 'the system' for stage-managing the demonstration against her.

Following the trial, the Mangaliso's three children went to live with their maternal grandmother, Mrs Grace Qunta. Timo Bezuidenhoud, who had been chief administrator of Cape Town's black townships for many years and was a friend of Mrs Mangaliso, was appointed curator responsible for the children's portion of their father's estate.

Lindi Mangaliso is incarcerated in Pollsmoor prison.

On 4 March, 1989, Shelini and Peter were reprieved and had their death sentences commuted to 20 years imprisonment by the Acting State President, Mr Chris Heunis.

In August 1985, an anonymous letter addressed to 'Lean' was found in the cell Shelini was being held in along with some other men. The letter said:

'If you can get me out of this place I really don't know what I will do for you. Please Dear try all you can. Those people must die before the 13th. and I will pay.

'Also the court books must be missing. If your brother can kill these people I will be a free man. Even my cell-mate with this woman they are throwing everything at me. Here are the names of these people: Nxawe, Julius Tshaka, Leonard Knipe (he is a white man).'*

A handwriting expert identified Mbuzeli Shelini as the author of the letter.

** Julius Tshaka was reputedly in the house when the murder took place. Shelini implicated him in the crime but he was not charged.*

22.
TWO RUTHLESS KILLERS

(YASSIEM HARRIS AND SANDRA SMITH: 1986)

On 1 September, 1986, Mrs Sandra Smith (22) and her lover, Yassiem Harris (19), throttled and stabbed to death Jermaine Abrahams, a sixteen year-old school-girl, at her Mitchell's Plain home.

Sandra Smith and Yassiem Harris first met in 1983. At the time, Smith, who was married and had two children, lived with her parents in Mitchell's Plain. Her husband was a fisherman who was away at sea for long periods of time but sent money home on a regular basis. Harris lived nearby.

One day in September or October 1983, Harris received a note and some money from Smith. The note said that she wanted to meet him in a park. At the subsequent meeting she told him how much she 'admired' him. 'She also asked if I wanted to sleep over because her husband had left with the ship,' Harris said. 'The first night I got into bed with her and that's how the relationship started.'

Yassiem Harris was almost 17-years-old when he met Sandra Smith. He smoked dagga, took mandrax and had been a juvenile delinquent since the age of 13. He had left school at fifteen while in Standard 6, in order to get a job to supplement the family income. His first job was working alongside his father at a car-sound specialist in Claremont, Cape Town, but he was dismissed after six months when it was discovered that he had stolen R10 000 in cash, and cheques totalling R26 000. He was convicted and received six cuts with the cane. The hiding, his father claimed, 'made no impression on him'.

From that point on, Harris' gradual descent into a life of unemployment and crime became almost inevitable. He drifted from job to job, became a member of a gang called the *Hard Livings* and, not long afterwards, was arrested a second time for breaking into a school. He got another six cuts but that also 'did not make any impression on him,' his father said.

Harris secretly slept with Smith every night at her parents' home, and not long after they met she started giving him money. 'It was, I would say, to attract my attention,' Harris explained. 'Sometimes it was R100, R50 or R80.'

Not surprisingly, he soon gave up any pretence of looking for work.

After they had been seeing each other for about six months, their relationship faced its first crisis when Phillip Smith, Sandra's husband, returned from sea and learnt of his wife's affair from some neighbours. He responded by getting help from three of his friends to beat Harris up, but no sooner had he gone back to sea than Harris and his wife were together again.

Even though the two of them were virtually living as man and wife, this did not prevent Harris from pursuing other women. Some mornings he used to loiter outside local high schools before school started, chatting to the school girls and making dates for the afternoon. This was how he got to know Jermaine Abrahams and learnt where she lived.

The affair between Harris and Smith continued for over two-and-a-half years. When Sandra's husband was ashore, they would stop seeing each other and then resume the relationship when he left for sea again. In 1985, Smith became pregnant for a third time and was uncertain whether the father was her husband or Harris.

The final tragic sequence of events which were to end with the death of Jermaine Abrahams, to some extent began in March 1986 when Phillip Smith returned home to find his wife and Harris together again. Harris fled to avoid being beaten for a second time, and Sandra followed him – abandoning her children in the process. As far as Phillip Smith was concerned, the marriage was over and so was the free supply of money he had been providing.

For a time after the break-up of her marriage, Sandra stayed with friends in Grassy Park then, with Harris' help, she found lodgings in Mitchell's Plain. But within a few months all her money had gone and things were becoming desperate.

Smith and Harris dabbled in video fraud – hiring video machines then selling them – but on the afternoon of 31 August, they discussed breaking into the Abrahams' house, tying up Jermaine, and then stealing goods. Harris suggested this particular house because he claimed to have broken into the place a year earlier and stolen a large amount of money. He saw no reason why they shouldn't find valuable property yet again. What was more, he knew that Mr and Mrs Abrahams usually left for work before 7 a.m. and that their daughter, Jermaine, left for school at about 7.40 a.m.

The next morning, they got up very early and walked to the Abrahams' house, arriving there around 7.30 a.m.. Harris knocked on the door and when Jermaine answered he asked if he could make a telephone call.

According to Smith, Harris did not introduce her to Jermaine and Jermaine asked him to go to her bedroom where she could speak to him. At first Smith sat in the front room – then she became impatient.

'I heard voices. I went to her bedroom because I wanted to see what was going on.

'Yassiem said: "Jermaine, Sandra and I are going to tie you up and steal things from the house. Don't tell your parents it was us.".

Photograph courtesy of *The Argus*

Sandra Smith and Yassiem Harris

Harris then locked the front door and put the key in his pocket. They then tied Jermaine up, but while she was on the bedroom floor lying on her stomach, someone knocked at the front door. She tried to scream for help and struggled to get free, but Harris clamped his hand over her mouth while Smith held her legs.

When the knocking stopped, Harris and Smith put a dishcloth around Jermaine's throat to throttle her 'so that she would become faint'.

'I didn't want to pull tight on my side,' Smith said.

According to Smith, Harris then went into the kitchen and returned wearing orange kitchen gloves and carrying a knife. Harris claimed the knife was lying on the dressing table and Smith picked it up and said, 'Stab her dead'.

'I just grabbed the knife out of her hand and started stabbing Jermaine continuously in the neck,' he said. 'She was lying on the floor on her stomach and as I was stabbing her, she wriggled on to her back but I still went on stabbing her.'

After the attack, Jermaine managed to get free and get to her feet. She took a few steps and fell over. She got up, staggered into the passage, and collapsed once more. (The police found a four-fingered print in blood on the door-frame of Jermaine's bedroom. This print was Jermaine's. A palm print which was later identified as belonging to Mrs Smith was found on the door of the main bedroom.

The position of Jermaine's print was consistent with her having attempted to break loose and grab the door. The knife which the police discovered at the scene held no fingerprints since it was 'one mass of blood'.)

Harris then carried Jermaine into her parents' bedroom. She told them where her mother's jewellery was hidden and begged for water.

'Yassiem, I don't want to die now,' she said.

While Harris stood over Jermaine, Smith looked under the wardrobe which Jermaine indicated. After Smith had found the valuables, she handed them to Harris and then began a systematic search of the cupboards. She saw that the duvet had been pulled over Jermaine's head and it was then she realized Harris had slit Jermaine's throat.

After Jermaine was dead, they collected the items they wanted to steal, and with Harris wearing a pair of tracksuit pants to cover the blood on his trousers they made their escape.

Two weeks later, while Smith was being questioned by the police regarding a video machine that she and Harris had hired and sold, she suddenly confessed to the killing of Jermaine Abrahams.

'I wouldn't have been able to live with it,' she said. Then she wept and under cross-examination admitted, 'He pulled the scarf tight across her mouth and then cut her throat.'

On 15 September, Sandra Smith was charged with the murder of Jermaine Abrahams. Five days later, Yassiem Harris was arrested and charged similarly.

Smith and Harris appeared at a preliminary hearing at the Mitchell's Plain Magistrates' Court on 23 September. They pleaded guilty to murder, alternatively culpable homicide, and to stealing R2 000 worth of jewellery.

In a statement made to the court, Smith said: 'Mr Harris and I went to the Abrahams' house, knocked on the door and the girl answered. We tied her up and tried to throttle her with dischloths from the kitchen. But she would not die. He started to stab her, but still she wouldn't die.

'She kept on pleading with us to let her live. She said she didn't want to die.

'We then took her to her mother's bedroom – she said there was valuable jewellery there. She showed us where it was and we took it out.

'Then she started to get weaker. We put her on the bed. She was getting cold and asked us for water. We didn't give it to her. She started to bleed more and died. He slit her throat.'

'Did you want her to die?" the Magistrate asked.

'Not really. Mr Harris started to feel sorry for her afterwards but she would have been able to identify us.'

As she was leaving the court handcuffed to Harris, Smith had tears streaming down her face. When she saw her mother in the crowd she shouted, 'Mummy they didn't give me bail ... Mummy, get me out of here...'.

A month later, Smith and Harris were sent to Valkenberg Hospital for 30 days' psychiatric evaluation. Although Harris was said to have an 'anti-social personality disorder', both he and Smith were judged fit to stand trial.

The trial of Sandra Smith and Yassiem Harris began at the Cape Town Supreme Court on 1 December, 1986. Both were accused of murdering and robbing Jermaine Abrahams.

During the trial, both Smith and Harris attempted to shift the onus of blame on to the other. Smith maintained that Harris had done the actual killing and Harris claimed to have been dominated by Smith. Neither denied being party to the murder. However, when the exact nature of their relationship was examined, it was found that neither Harris nor Smith dominated the other. In other words, they were both equally responsible for their actions.

During the trial, some love letters which the accused had written to each other were read out in court – a fact which seemed to embarrass Mrs Smith more than the accusation of murder laid against her. In one letter in particular, she had referred to their sexually-satisfying relationship and said,

> *'I will never sleep with another man, not even with my own husband because during five years he could not please me. That is why I felt so sad this morning when you said you were pleased no one was waiting for you. What about me? Where do I really stand with you? I love you and I don't want to lose you. Yassiem, please tell me I must wait for you. I want you to believe that we will be together because I do. The way our sex has been, I don't believe I will ever again get a man who can please me so. That is why I am going to wait till you come out.'*

Harris said in a letter:

> *'I want to tell you to forget me because I don't no if it will be the same when I come out one day. I love you very much Sandra you no it, but I don't no what's going to happen in such a long time.'*

On 11 December, 1986, both Smith and Harris were convicted of murder and robbery with aggravating circumstances.

During his two-hour summing-up the Judge-President, Mr Justice Munnik, described Harris, who had tried to put the blame on Smith by saying he had acted on her instructions, as 'an appalling witness'. It was clear, the Judge maintained, that Harris had wielded the knife throughout and his parrot-like repetition of 'I don't know' when repeatedly asked why he killed the girl was merely a ploy. It was equally obvious that Harris had killed the girl to prevent her identifying them. Furthermore, his claim to have been dominated by Smith was refuted by the psychiatrist. Smith was demanding but not dominant, and there was no evidence to indicate that she pressurized Harris into committing any crimes that he would not normally commit. Indeed, the judge concluded, both Smith and Harris helped each other throughout and were equally responsible for what followed.

On 22 December, Smith and Harris were sentenced to hang because they had jointly 'planned and ruthlessly executed' the murder of Jermaine Abrahams. (Harris was also sentenced to 10 years in prison for robbery with aggravating circumstances. Smith was sentenced to 7 years.) When the death sentence was handed down, Smith became hysterical and had to be taken struggling and wailing to the cells.

Sandra Smith and Yassiem Harris were executed on 2 June, 1989, at the Pretoria Central Prison.

23.

THE RISE AND FALL OF 'MR COOL'

(ZOLA MAHOBE: 1983–87)

From 1983 to 1987, Zola Mahobe was perhaps the most well-known black businessman in the country. To Sowetans he was 'Mr Cool' – a larger-than-life character who, from humble beginnings, had turned himself into a jet-setting multi-millionaire, bought a soccer team in the process, and steered it to the top of Division One in the National Soccer League.

Today, Zola Mahobe is in prison serving a sixteen-year sentence for bank fraud involving R6-million. This is his story.

Zola Mahobe was born in Sophiatown, and attended secondary school at Meadowlands High in Soweto. After leaving school in 1971, he worked for an international company in Johannesburg for ten years. In 1981, he joined a computer company for just over a year and then, in 1983, started his own business: *Power Promotions*.

From that point on, his rise to the top was truly meteoric. One minute no-one had heard of Zola Mahobe, and the next his name seemed to be on everybody's lips. He was seen at all the best places. There were plush restaurants, expensive cars, palatial houses, overseas travel, racehorses ... indeed, all the trappings of success. And though Mahobe was married and had two children, he was always accompanied by his mistress, Snowy Tebelo Moshoeshoe, a checking clerk who worked for the Standard Bank.

In 1985, thirty-one year-old Mahobe bought *Mamelodi Sundowns* soccer team, reputedly for R100 000. Then, in his determination to take the team to the top of the league, he went on another spending spree. Over the next two years, it was estimated that he spent over R2-million on the club. He paid record fees for the country's top players and rewarded his new signings with expensive gifts, including top-of-the-range BMW cars. Suddenly, *Mamelodi Sundowns* were a force to be reckoned with alongside *Kaiser Chiefs* and *Orlando Pirates*.

And, while *Mamelodi Sundowns* were going from strength to strength, Mahobe's business empire was also expanding. Before too long, he owned butcheries, bottle stores and a travel agency, all of which he ran from his offices in Eloff Street.

'I have made a lot of ground in business because I don't hesitate when I want something,' he said.

Mahobe earned a reputation for being a generous man – he treated his employees well and even set his friends up in well-paid positions – and was extremely popular in the community. His motto was: 'Let everybody be happy then the money will flow in.' In May 1986, for example, he took the entire *Mamelodi Sundowns* team, plus wives and girlfriends – a total of 53 people – on an all-expenses paid trip to the FA Cup Final in London.

It was only later that people would realise that all the extravagance was being paid for by someone else.

In the end, it was simple greed that brought Zola Mahobe to book.

While on a trip to West Germany in May 1987, Mahobe became consumed by an 'insatiable' desire to own a Mercedes Benz 500SEL. He seemed to think that although he had a number of other luxury cars, this particular model would signify that he had finally 'arrived'. Because of the weak rand exchange rate, it was suggested that it would be better for him to buy the car in South Africa. To facilitate the deal, Mercedes in Germany contacted its agents in South Africa. In turn, Mahobe's bank – the Standard Bank – was notified of the impending transaction. Normally, a credit enquiry of this nature would go through Miss Snowy Moshoeshoe, but on this occasion she happened to be on leave and the true state of Mahobe's accounts emerged.

A police investigation was instituted after an internal audit of Mahobe's accounts on 20 May revealed the real nature of his financial affairs.

For five years, Miss Moshoeshoe had been fraudulently passing credit transfer forms without substantiating cheques, and depositing them into Mahobe's accounts. In this way, she falsely created credit balances which were offset by a debit through inter-bank transactions.

Snowy Moshoeshoe had aided and abetted her lover to squander over R10-million!

Miss Moshoeshoe had first met Mahobe in 1976, when she was still a schoolgirl writing matric. He was the first man in her life. Later they became lovers, but Moshoeshoe remained faithful to him, even after she learnt that he was a married man with two daughters. So strong was his influence on her that she tolerated his promises that she would one day be his legal wife.

Immediately after the discovery, Miss Moshoeshoe was arrested and charged with fraud involving R7,7-million. At the time, she was earning R700 a month and living with her family in a municipal house in Soweto. Two-and-a-half months later she was convicted of 129 cases of fraud and sentenced to 10 years in prison.

'I did not want to disappoint him and made transfers whenever he wanted money,' she said.

Zola Mahobe, meanwhile, had vanished.

At first, the Standard Bank offered a reward of R10 000 for any information which led to Mahobe's arrest. This was later increased to R50 000. Nevertheless, Mahobe remained a fugitive for almost nine months. He was finally arrested in Gaborone by the Botswana police (at the request of the South African Police) and handed over to the South African authorities.

In the interim, both his own and Miss Moshoeshoe's estates had been sequestrated. His wife, Mrs Siza Mahobe, and his two children, Mondi (9) and Beybey (2), were destitute after their house had been sold by the bank in an attempt to recoup its losses.

Zola Mahobe's trial began at the Johannesburg Regional Court on 8 July, 1988. He was charged with five counts of theft involving R6 037 870 of the R10 315 000 allegedly taken from the bank. The five charges related to 93 fraudulent transactions that took place between 3 February, 1983 and 9 May, 1987.

Mahobe pleaded not guilty.

He claimed that when he withdrew money from his accounts he did not know that it had been fraudulently deposited by Miss Moshoeshoe. It was his belief, he maintained, that Miss Moshoeshoe had received the money from farms and properties sold in Lesotho by her relatives, headed by King Moshoeshoe.

On 12 January, 1989, the Magistrate, Mr A.B. Booysens sentenced Zola Mahobe to a total of 29 years in prison after finding him guilty on all five counts of theft. Thirteen years of the sentence were to run concurrently, giving Mahobe an effective 16 years imprisonment.

In his summing-up to a jam-packed courtroom, Mr Booysens said that Mahobe's claim that he thought the funds put into his various business bank accounts were a loan from the Moshoeshoe family as 'false beyond reasonable doubt'. The magistrate also pointed out that whereas Miss Moshoeshoe had shown remorse for her actions, Mahobe had pleaded not guilty and shown no remorse. He also discounted Mahobe's explanation that he had remained in Botswana for eight months after charges were laid against him in South Africa because he was 'sick from the shock' as 'far-fetched'.

Despite the court's findings, a number of *Mamelodi Sundowns* supporters raged against the sentence which they claimed was 'unfair'. One supporter maintained that Mahobe should have been given the opportunity to repay the money. 'This was the harshest sentence I have ever heard of,' he said. And another claimed that, 'the worst he should have been given was a suspended sentence.'

The sentence stood. 'Mr Cool' had finally been stripped of his title.

24.

THE SCREWDRIVER RAPIST

(WILLIAM FREDERICH VAN DER MERWE)

No-one knows what turns a man into a rapist, although there is no shortage of theories. Some criminologists believe that men with exaggerated or even mildly accentuated sex drives become either *Don Juans* or rapists. In other words, intelligent, virile men satisfy their needs through guile and persuasion, while others resort to prostitutes, pornography or force.

Some rapists commit the crime because the opportunity presents itself, while others carefully plan and premeditate their actions. The worst sex criminals are those where rape is accompanied by sadistic murder. In these cases, rape does not flow primarily from a physiological sexual basis but is motivated by other causes. For some rapists, the act is motivated by a desire to dominate.

William Frederich van der Merwe fell into this latter category. He raped women because he enjoyed the feeling of power that it gave him. His desire was to take revenge upon society and women in particular – in the end he would resort to murder.

Van der Merwe was born in Kew, Johannesburg, in December 1951. Mary, his mother, was a devout Catholic. Thomas, his father, worked as a driver for the Johannesburg tramways.

When William was fifteen months-old, his father was killed in a motorcycle accident. Seven weeks later, his mother gave birth to John, her tenth child.

The death of Thomas van der Merwe was a catastrophe of untold proportions. Money had always been short for the family, but now they were destitute. In desperation, Mary turned to the authorities for help. She received some assistance from the Society of Vincent de Paul, a local charity, but the money was never enough. Worse still for William was the fact that his mother, apparently acting out of a misguided sense of guilt that her youngest son had never known a father, lavished more affection on John than on him. Not only did William grow up in abject poverty, but his situation was exacerbated by the fact that he felt unloved and utterly rejected.

When William was two years-old, the family was split up. William and John were sent to a children's home in Pretoria. Four of their brothers and sisters went to a Johannesburg children's home, and the four eldest stayed with their mother. William was devastated by the move, but worse was still to come. When his sixteen year-old sister married, she came to collect John to take him to live with her and her husband. William then knew that he had finally been abandoned. Anger and resentment took hold of his soul.

At the age of six, William went to live with his mother who had moved into a council house in Bertrams, Johannesburg, and attended Bertram's Junior School. It was quickly realised that he had a severe learning handicap and behavioural problems. After the principal had noted that there was something 'radically wrong' with William, he was examined by a psychiatrist. Although he was judged to have an IQ of 90, he was still unable to read or write. This failing had a negative effect on him and he became cheeky, aggressive and noisy. He was eventually diagnosed as dyslexic and sent for special classes at a nearby clinic. It was later discovered that he was using the bus-fare he had been given to go to the cinema. He was seven years of age.

As Van der Merwe grew older, things got worse – not better. He was ridiculed by his classmates for his inability to read or write and gave vent to his anger by turning to crime. He would later admit to committing his first robbery – the theft of a teacher's purse – while still in Standard 1.

'I can't read the words,' he once told his mother. 'The teacher just ignores me. The other children laugh at me. I'm not interested. I don't want to go to school.'

Not long afterwards, Van der Merwe began breaking into houses on a regular basis. He was eventually caught, and in August 1965, he was sentenced to three cuts for housebreaking and theft. At 13 he was a registered thief. Two years later, he was caught stealing again, but this time the court sentenced him to reform school and he was sent to Tokai Reformatory in the Cape.

After being at reform school for about eighteen months, Van der Merwe ran away and went to live with his sister, Flora, and her husband. They gave him a job in their carpet-laying business, and for a while he lived a fairly normal life. It was during this period that he also met a girl at the church guild and fell in love for the first time. Although the girl was pregnant when they first met, they became very close and for some time virtually lived together. Unfortunately, Van der Merwe regarded the relationship as much more serious than she did. He later learnt that the girl was seeing other boyfriends and the affair ended after a violent argument. For Van der Merwe it was the final humiliation: a horrible, pathetic ending to a hopeless relationship.

According to Van der Merwe, the urge to rape first occurred in Vereeniging when one day he saw a pretty girl in the street and tried to chat to her. She was unresponsive. At that moment, he claimed, all the anger and resentment he felt against society came bubbling to the surface. Almost without thinking, he pulled out a knife and flashed it under the girl's nose. He saw a terrible look of fear come into her eyes. He had never known such power before.

After that incident, he approached other girls. He would follow them and in lifts and other secluded places, would either exhibit himself, make indecent suggestions, or actively touch them. At first, he did not wish to hurt any of the girls, but merely overawe and impress them with a sense of masculinity and power.

Eventually, he was spotted in the street by one of his victims and taken to the police. In May 1971, Van der Merwe, then aged 19, was convicted on two accounts of attempted assault and one of attempted rape. He was given a suspended prison sentence, placed in the custody of his sister, and ordered to undergo treatment for dyslexia. Rape gave Van der Merwe a sense of power he had never experienced before. His self-esteem was very low, partly because he was ridiculed for neither being able to read nor write. In treating his dyslexia, it was hoped that his self-esteem would improve and his desire to rape diminish.

It was only a few months later that Van der Merwe finally went over the edge. Between September and November 1971, he raped at least nine women. It was also during this period that he exchanged the knife that he habitually carried for a screwdriver. The press quickly labelled him the 'Screwdriver Rapist'.

Van der Merwe often used the same *modus operandi*: he would dress in white overalls and visit women's homes, claiming to be an electrician. In one case, when he raped a young mother after threatening her and her child, he lured her into the bedroom by asking her where the plug in that room was. In another, he tried to rape a student whom he gagged and tied to her bed. He tried to stop her screaming by breaking an empty wine bottle over her head but when she carried on shouting, he ran away. He also raped a pretty 14-year-old schoolgirl after gagging her and threatening her with a screwdriver. Regarding this particular case, Mr Justice Steyn, the man who would preside over Van der Merwe's subsequent trial would say: 'This is one of the grimmest cases of rape I have known in 15 years on the Bench. It is difficult to be objective in this case. A young and very attractive girl – a virgin until she was ravaged by Van der Merwe... This is the kind of person I am going to protect.'

Van der Merwe eventually gave himself up to the police after being confronted by his sister and her husband. She had read that the rapist had been seen in a blue kombi – the same type of vehicle which Van der Merwe drove. Once in police custody, Van der Merwe co-operated fully with the authorities and was sent to Sterkfontein Mental Hospital for 28 days observation, after which he was pronounced fit to stand trial.

On 28 February, 1972, he appeared at a summary trial at the Rand Supreme Court. He was charged with five counts of rape and four of attempted rape, theft and *crimen injuria*. On 22 March, 1972, he was sentenced to death by Mr Justice Steyn.

'I knew I was going to get the death penalty,' Van der Merwe would later claim. 'I saw it in his face.'

Van der Merwe's legal counsel immediately appealed against the sentence and on 2 June, 1973, an Appeal Court sitting in Bloemfontein handed down its judgment. By a vote of two to one, Van der Merwe's death sentence was commuted to 20 years in prison.

The dissenting judge, Mr Chief Justice Ogilvie Thompson, disagreed with the decision. He said at the time: 'Having regard to the number and the premediated nature of these crimes, and to the degree of criminality consistently exhibited over a considerable period, I remain unpersuaded that the sentence imposed by the court is inappropriate.'

Fortunately for Van der Merwe, the other two appeal judges did not share Mr Chief Justice Ogilvie Thompson's point of view. Mr Justice Holmes, one of the other judges maintained: 'What this youth needs imperatively is a good spell of discipline and training. Society does not require his extermination.'

For the next fifteen years, William van der Merwe was locked away in prison, where he underwent a rehabilitation programme and received drug therapy. On 1 March, 1987, he was granted parole and released from the Zonderwater Prison in Pretoria. The first knowledge the general public would have of his release would be early in 1989.

At about 5 p.m. on the evening of 4 January, 1989, Christine Lennon (27) and Theresa Mizen (19) were hitch-hiking to Tamboerskloof after a day at Muizenberg beach. They were picked up outside Burger Fair on Main Road, Tokai, by Van der Merwe, who was driving a white Mazda bakkie. (It would later turn out that Van der Merwe carried in his bakkie three sets of handcuffs, rope, rubber gloves, several varieties of exotic condoms, various 'sexual aids' and 29 screwdrivers in a toolbox.)

According to Theresa, 'The driver was a white male. He spoke fluent English and appeared to be a respectable person. I sat in the middle. We said we were going to Cape Town. He said he was too, but had to go to Constantia to pick up some papers first.'

Van der Merwe drove to a house in Constantia and went around the back. Moments later, he came around to the passenger-side door and pointed a gun at his two victims. He ordered them to climb into the back of the bakkie, where he hand-cuffed them and tied their feet. He said that if they did exactly as he told them, they would still be alive when he had finished. Fifteen minutes later, he stopped in a deserted part of Constantia forest. When he unlocked the back of the bakkie, he said to Theresa, 'If you scream, I'll cut off her [Christine's] breasts in front of you. Yours too.'

He took off all his clothes, commented upon their 'pretty breasts', and then raped Theresa.

Afterwards, he gave both girls a cigarette, chatted with them, and promised not to do either of them any harm.

'He said he just wanted some fun with us then he'd drop us off somewhere and we could get home on our own.'

However, he forced the two girls back into the bakkie and drove around 'for what seemed like hours'. (Their final destination was Grabouw forest about forty kilometres out of the city.)

Eventually, Van der Merwe stopped the bakkie and raped Miss Lennon in front of her friend and then he made her walk with him into the bushes.

At first Miss Mizen thought of trying to run away but with her feet tied together and her hands cuffed behind her back she knew that escape was impossible. Then she saw his trousers...

'I grabbed them and got the pistol. The moment I felt the metal in my hand I prayed, 'God, please let there be bullets in it.'

Although she had never handled a gun before in her life she managed to cock the pistol. She lay in wait until some time later when she heard Van der Merwe approaching.

'I heard his footsteps,' she said. 'He was alone. I saw the knife in his hand and I knew I'd never see Christine again.'

(When the police arrived later, they found Christine Lennon lying among some pine needles nearby in a pool of her own blood. She had been stabbed to death.)

As Van der Merwe came around the back of the vehicle, she rolled on to her side and pulled the trigger. She heard Van der Merwe give a sigh and saw him fall. The bullet had hit him in the head. She wriggled to the back of the bakkie and fired another shot, this time hitting him in the shoulder. When she tried to shoot him for a third time, the gun jammed.

Shaking with terror, she managed to find a knife in the van, cut the ropes around her ankles, and make her way to a nearby road. A passing motorist took her to the police station.

Van der Merwe was taken to hospital where he died a few hours later without regaining consciousness. The reign of terror of the Screwdriver Rapist had finally ended.

Miss Mizen will have to live with the horror of that afternoon for the rest of her life, but for Van der Merwe she feels no sorrow. Her words are perhaps a fitting epitaph for a brutal psychopath.

'There was nothing. There is nothing. It was as if it had nothing to do with me. I did not even feel he got his just deserts...'

The author comments:
The case of William van der Merwe raises a number of alarming issues, not least of which is how a dangerous maniac, a habitual criminal who is an acknowledged menace to society, can gain release from prison fifteen years after being sentenced to death for a series of horrendous crimes.

The authorities maintain that Van der Merwe's parole was supervised in a 'professional and competent' manner. This is no doubt true, yet Van der Merwe raped and murdered an innocent young woman after his release from prison. Surely this is a clear indication that there is something wrong with the system of assessing the mental health of a convicted rapist.

Unfortunately, psychiatry is not an exact science, and society has the right to be protected from individuals such as William van der Merwe. Until a more effective method of assessment to determine the success or failure of an individual's rehabilitation programme is devised, it is widely felt that the public has every right to demand that such individuals be kept out of circulation – permanently if necessary.

25. THE STRIJDOM SQUARE MASSACRE

(BAREND HENDRIK STRYDOM: 1988)

On the afternoon of 15 November, 1988, twenty-three year-old Barend Hendrik Strydom donned camouflage-style army fatigue, loaded his 9 mm pistol, and set out for central Pretoria. His pockets bulged: he was carrying a further two magazines and 200 loose bullets.

At around 3 p.m. he parked his car in Prinsloo Street and walked to Strijdom Square – specially chosen for its links to Prime Minister J.G. Strijdom, who had strong *apartheid* ideals – and began shooting any black person who got in his way.

After shooting one man outside the State Theatre, he crossed Church Street and headed towards Prinsloo Street. On the corner of Church and Prinsloo Streets, he shot two more people. One of his victims was a man standing in the street; another a woman sitting inside a taxi. Strydom carried on walking down Prinsloo Street.

'It was important to keep moving during the operation to keep the element of surprise', he explained. 'I ran and looked around searching for blacks. I did not look at their faces...'.

After walking three blocks, shooting a number of innocent pedestrians as he went, Strydom turned down Struben Street and entered Sato Engineering. He went over to a counter and began to reload a magazine.

At this point, Mr Simon Mukondoleli (32), who had bravely followed Strydom into the shop pretending to be a customer, walked up and tapped him on the shoulder.

'Excuse me *baas*, but that *baas* is calling you,' he said.

When Strydom looked round, Mr Mukondoleli snatched the gun from the counter and pointed it at him.

Strydom raised his hands. 'You've got me,' he said.

The two men then walked out into the street together where several policemen arrested Strydom.

'I am king of the *Wit Wolwe,*' Strydom said, just before being taken away in a police car.

That afternoon, Pretoria saw a smiling Strydom murder eight people and wound a further sixteen – many of them seriously.

'The shootings were to show the world that there are *boere* in the southern part of Africa who will fight to protect what is theirs,' Strydom said.

At the police station, after being told that he had killed five or six people, he replied: 'I shot badly'.

'He said that he felt nothing for the victims,' Lieutenant Viljoen, the investigating officer, said.

■

By the time Hendrik Strydom was sixteen he was already a member of a number of extremist right-wing organisations and had visions of an all-white nation being established in South Africa.

He claimed to have attended a *veld* school in Standard 8, where he had been warned against the communist system as well as drug and alchohol abuse.

'We were taught to be proud of our country,' he said. 'I began to read many books on politics in South Africa and also attended right-wing meetings. They were the only true political movements – unlike the Nationalist government which lies to the people.'

He saw some of the reform movements introduced by the government as a 'sell-out'. His views were encouraged by his father, Mr Nic Strydom, an ex-policeman, an elder in the Nederduits Hervormde Kerk, and a former regional leader of the Heidelberg Afrikaaner Weerstandsbeweging (AWB).

Mr Nic Strydom would later claim proudly in court that he had 'planted the seeds of religion and right-wing political views' in his son's heart. He also maintained that his son was a dedicated church-goer and a person who strongly believed in God.

'I explained to him that, according to the Bible, each nation should have its own church and religion, which Hendrik accepted wholeheartedly.'

It was also Mr Strydom's belief that 'blacks were animals'.

'Blacks are not human beings according to the Bible, and many books I have read, and in my eyes they are animals. Many books Hendrik and I have read state, among other things, that Jews of today are not whites, blacks are animals and all whites stem from the Israelites,' Mr Strydom added.

His son claimed that as a result of his political involvement and dedication to the Herstigte Nationale Party, the Conservative Party and the AWB, his school work had suffered and his marks had deteriorated. After matriculating in 1984, he joined the police force.

'I became more aware of the enemy, especially people belonging to the left-wing organizations such as the United Democratic Front and the so-called Workers Union and their affiliated organizations, which were all African National Congress front movements.'

He saw the actions which the government was taking to combat internal rebellion as ineffective and began to fear that South Africa was 'going to the communists'.

'My interest in politics stems from an internal fear that for myself as a young man, the government could not ensure a good future and the older generation were becoming tired of fighting the enemy.'

After graduating from police college, Strydom was stationed at Nigel. On one occasion he saw the corpse of a white nurse who had been killed during a riot. This made a marked impression on him and served to confirm his worst fears: the country was at war and blacks, who threatened the survival of whites, were the 'enemy'. Indeed, as far as he was concerned, blacks threatened the survival of all on the planet. 'There has been a decrease in the oxygen level in central Africa because blacks removed the trees there,' he maintained.

Some time later, he attended a motorcar accident in which a black man had been decapitated. He had a photograph of himself taken holding the man's head aloft and had wanted the picture – plus the words 'ANC beware!' – printed in the police magazine, *Servamus*. He was prevented from doing this and not long afterwards was investigated by the security branch regarding his involvement in right-wing politics.

'I was approached by the security branch about 30 times,' Strydom said.

It was in the latter half of 1988, that he decided to take matters into his own hands.

A week before the Strijdom Square massacre, Strydom visited the Voortrekker Monument to pray and re-enact the Blood River vow.

'I prayed and asked the Lord to show his will and to see I was not hindered in carrying out the deeds...'

That night, he drove to Wheeler's Farm squatter camp at De Deur near Vereeniging, where he shot dead one woman and wounded another. This was a 'practice run' he maintained, to see if he was 'mentally and physically capable' of shooting people.

After the shooting, he camped on a farm at Heidelberg where he prayed and meditated for two days. He did this, he said, to see if God was happy with his plan or not.

'I got no sign to indicate I must not carry on,' he added.

Four days later, he drove into central Pretoria and shot dead eight innocent people.

The so-called *Wit Wolf* trial began on Monday, 15 May, 1989, at the Pretoria Supreme Court. The courtroom was packed to capacity on every day of the nine-day hearing and large crowds, marshalled by a contingent of riot police, gathered outside the courthouse.

Strydom was charged with eight counts of murder, 16 charges of attempted murder, and one of pointing a firearm.

He pleaded not guilty.

On the first two days, the State called a number of witnesses to the stand but no-one appeared for the defence. (By the end of the trial 33 people had appeared for the State and 4 for the defence).

On Wednesday, 17 May, Mr Justice Louis Harms found Strydom guilty on all counts and called for arguments in mitigation of sentence.

'I see what I did as totally correct,' Strydom declared the following day. 'If I had to do it again I would do the same thing'.

When questioned about the *Wit Wolwe* movement, Strydom maintained that it had been established in February 1986, but would give no further details. The police claimed that investigations indicated that the *Wit Wolwe* was merely a figment of Strydom's imagination. When it was put to the accused that he was bragging in an attempt to make himself important, Strydom denied this.

On 25 May, the day Mr Justice Harms was to pass sentence, Court C was packed with Strydom's family, friends and supporters – including an elderly couple in traditional Voortrekker dress – over an hour before Strydom was due to appear. When he was finally brought up from the cells, he was warmly greeted by well-wishers. His stepmother, Mrs Daphne Strydom, after embracing him, kissed him on the cheek and said proudly: *'Jy's 'n boer'* (You're a farmer).

Strydom, the self-styled leader of the *Wit Wolwe*, was sentenced to death eight times.

A short gasp was the only sound heard in the courtroom when sentence was passed. Minutes later, Strydom was whisked away to the Pretoria Central Prison.

Outside the courthouse, a smiling Mrs Strydom told waiting pressmen that she 'felt good' and was proud of being a *boer*. '*Die Vierkleur hoog,*' (The *Vierkleur* is high) she cried. (The *Vierkleur* was the name of the flag of the independent *boer* republic called for in the Transvaal in the late nineteenth century.)

Most of the people waiting outside the court believed the sentence to be appropriate and just. One onlooker, Mr Jospeh Mongale of Soshanguve, claimed that the outcome of the trial would restore faith in South Africa's judicial system. The outcome was fair and most expected just that, he said. Miss Belina Khumalo, one of Strydom's victims, said that she thought justice had been done.

Many people saw parallels between the Strydom trial and that of another famous 'patriot', Sydney Robert Leibbrandt.

In 1943, Sydney Robert Leibbrandt, a boer rebel, was sentenced to death for treason. Although Leibbrandt refused to give evidence at any stage in the trial, he claimed he had acted for 'Volk and Fuhrer' and gave the Nazi salute when he first entered the court, to which several spectators responded. After being sentenced to death, Leibbrandt shouted loudly and clearly, 'I greet death!'

(Strydom acknowledged Leibbrandt as one of his heroes.)

On a more cautionary note, however, Mr M. Motsheka, the Transvaal chairman of the National Association of Democratic Lawyers, declared: 'He is a victim of *apartheid* and the crimes he committed and the sentence imposed on him are the product of *apartheid*. Sentencing Strydom to death will not cure the evil of *apartheid*.'

In a press interview given a few days after the sentencing, Mr Nic Strydom told reporters: 'I'm proud of Hendrik because he sacrificed himself for his beliefs. He is an honest man and I respect him for that. He killed for love – the love of a nation.'

On 2 February, 1990, the South African government declared a moratorium on capital punishment. No executions have been carried out since that date.

Hendrik Strydom is at present on death row awaiting news of his fate.

■

- On 27 May, 1989, Mr Simon Mukondoleli was presented with a R3 000 reward by the police for his heroic action in disarming Strydom and preventing further loss of life. Mr Mkondeleli received a number of death threats for his effort.

- On 2 October, 1989, Strydom became engaged to Miss Karin Rautenbach, a twenty-two year-old final-year student at Pretoria Teachers Training College. The romance started with an exchange of letters after Strydom's conviction and sentence. Miss Rautenbach put the engagement ring on her own finger since she was separated from her fiance by a glass partition.

  Strydom and Rautenbach were married on 27 November, 1989, while Strydom was on death row at Pretoria Central Prison. After the twenty-minute ceremony, the couple were allowed their first physical contact – in the presence of a prison warder. After their 'half-hour honeymoon' Strydom was returned to his cell.

When the new Mrs Strydom was asked how she felt about not being able to have children, she said, 'As things stand now, a black majority rule is inevitable. We must accept that black revolutionaries will seek revenge like in most former colonies. When that happens I do not want my children to fall prey to them. Without complete freedom and self-government for white people of this country there is no future for the next generation.'

Mrs Trudy Rautenbach, the bride's mother, was proud of her daughter. Her son-in-law was, 'a fine *boer* boy full of character', she said.

After an internal investigation at Pretoria Teachers' Training College into Karin's activities, no action was taken against her.

- In July 1990, bomb attacks were made against the home and business premises of Democratic Party councillor, Mr Clive Gilbert, the home of an National Party member of the Johannesburg City Council, Mr Jan Burger, and on a synagogue in Rosettenville. An English-speaking man who contacted the *Citizen* newspaper claimed that the *Wit Wolwe* were responsible.

26.

THE 3-IN-A-BED MURDER

(MARIA KREBS: 1987)

At about 10 p.m. on the evening of 21 October, 1987, Miss Beverly Gaskin, the receptionist at Playmates Escort Agency in downtown Johannesburg, received a telephone call from a woman who said she had given her husband a surprise party and wanted a 'lady' for him.

Miss Gaskin asked how many ladies the caller wanted. The caller said she wanted only one and that she was going to sit and watch them.

Miss Gaskin then asked the caller for her name and address. 'Maria Krebs, 3 Munton Terrace, Bedfordview,' she was told. After confirming these details in the telephone directory, Miss Gaskin phoned back to say that she would be sending along a girl named 'Pat'.

'Pat's' real name was Miss Gertruida Magdalena du Preez. She was known to her friends as Linda.

The events that followed were to lead to one of the most sensational murder trials in South African legal history: the so-called 'three-in-a-bed' murder. It was also a night that 'Pat' du Preez and Maria Krebs will never forget.

According to Miss du Preez, she was taken to the house by her 'minder', George, who was paid R55. At the front door, she was greeted by Maria Krebs and her husband, Ralf. Ralf Krebs was wearing a dressing-gown and his wife a nightdress. The three of them went into the main bedroom where they drank wine together. While Ralf went to fetch another bottle, his wife explained to the call-girl that she (the call-girl) was her husband's birthday present.

When Ralf Krebs came in with the wine, he gave Miss du Preez a cash cheque for R120 and told her to first caress his wife and then have sex with him afterwards. He then took off his dressing-gown. Miss du Preez also removed some clothing so that she was dressed in a blouse, panties and shoes. Mrs Krebs was also naked.

'I kissed Mrs Krebs over her whole body. Then I kissed Mr Krebs over his whole body. Mrs Krebs sat behind me and kissed my back and breasts.'

After this, Krebs had intercourse with Miss du Preez in the presence of his wife. It was at this point in the proceedings, however, that things started to go disastrously wrong. The Krebs had a violent argument, and while Ralf was out of the room, Maria confided in Pat that she was going to kill her husband because he had 'slept around with Coloured women,' and had 'only married me for my money.'

Miss du Preez was alone in the bedroom when she heard a loud noise in another part of the house. Maria Krebs came back into the bedroom holding a pistol.

'She aimed the gun at me and pulled the trigger; there was a clicking sound,' the call-girl said.

Mrs Krebs went out again, locking the door behind her, but Miss du Preez used a telephone in the bedroom to phone the escort agency. She told them to send George for her because a woman was about to shoot someone. Before George arrived, she managed to get out of the house and ran to the house next door. It was just after midnight when the owner, Mr Chudleigh, answered the door.

'There was a young lady at the front door who asked me to phone the police as the lady next door was going to shoot her husband,' he said.

While he was on the telephone to the Brixton Murder and Robbery Squad, Du Preez left with her minder, George. About ten minutes later, Mr Chudleigh and his wife heard a noise which sounded like a door slamming.

'The next thing there was a rapping on one of the windows,' he said.

When they went to the patio, they saw Mrs Krebs sitting naked on a bench. After getting her a dressing-gown, Mr Chudleigh went to get a torch from his car and rushed across to the Krebs' house. Mrs Krebs had changed into one of her own dressing-gowns and was in the lounge speaking on the telephone to a friend. Ralf Krebs was lying in the hallway near the front door with a revolver next to him.

Mr Chudleigh pushed Mrs Krebs out of the way and telephoned for an ambulance, only to learn that his daughter had taken the initiative and had already called one.

Mrs Krebs went into the main bedroom where Mrs Chudleigh joined her, while Mr Chudleigh attended to the Krebs' two children, aged three and five years at the time.

'I spent the rest of the time trying to keep them in the main part of the house,' he said.

When Mr Chudleigh heard the ambulance in the street outside, he left the house to direct it to the house. When he looked for the revolver next to Mr Krebs' body, he found it had vanished. While the paramedics tried to revive Mr Krebs, the Bedfordview police arrived, and shortly afterwards a friend of Mrs Krebs.

A fireman, Mr Jan Liebenberg, went to speak to Mrs Krebs while the paramedics were busy with her husband.

'At that stage I did not tell her he was dead. I didn't think it was the right time. I told her we were still attending to her husband.' Mrs Krebs was crying. 'I hope the bastard dies,' she said. When she was later told that her husband was dead she replied, 'I didn't mean to shoot him...'.

■

The trial of Maria Krebs, who was accused of murdering her husband and attempting to murder 'Pat' du Preez, was held at the Rand Supreme Court in Johannesburg, early in March 1989. The presiding judge was Mr Justice D.O. Vermooten.

Photograph courtesy of *The Star*

Maria Krebs

The lurid descriptions of the events of 21 October, 1987 – a public glimpse into the private world of a call-girl – attracted intense public interest. There was also a small measure of controversy when it was discovered that Mrs Krebs' account of that fateful evening differed in certain key respects from that given by the prosecution's chief witness, 'Pat' du Preez.

According to Mrs Krebs, she spent an uneventful day shopping and collecting her children from school. When she returned home, she had a row with her husband because she had not accompanied him to a lawyer to sign bond papers for a new home they were buying. Then they had gone to the new house together and taken some video footage so that Mr Krebs could send the film to his parents who lived in Germany. Mrs Krebs said that they were happy and excited at this stage because they had something to look forward to.

When, at a later stage, her husband had asked what presents he should bring back with him from his forthcoming holiday in Germany, Mrs Krebs said that there was nothing they really needed or wanted, and that he should concentrate on the family first.

When asked by her defence counsel why she had raised this topic, Mrs Krebs lowered her head and began to sob quietly. Eventually she composed herself enough to explain that a week before, her husband had confessed to having an affair with another woman. She also found out that he had pubic lice.

Although she had been devastated at the time, she claimed that a few days later she had forgiven her husband.

On the evening of 21 October, 1987, they put their children to bed just before 8 p.m., watched the news, then went to bed themselves and had intercourse.

'My husband told me how much he loved me and I asked how he could hurt me; how he could go with other women?

'He told me love and sex were two different things and that he would prove to me they had nothing to do with one another.

'He told me we should get another lady. I didn't believe him because I had just made love to him.'

According to Mrs Krebs, her husband then dialled the Playmates Escort Agency and told her to say it was the Krebs' home and to ask for a lady to be sent for her husband.

'I thought it was a joke', she said.

When there was a knock at the door, her husband put on his dressing-gown, took some money from her purse, and went to answer. She remained in bed, naked under the duvet. He came back into the bedroom accompanied by Miss 'Pat' du Preez and wrote out a cheque for R120. He then suggested that Miss du Preez caress his wife and have sex with him afterwards.

'I was repulsed by the mere suggestion. I have never had a sexual relationship with a female.'

After taking off her clothes, Miss du Preez walked towards her.

'I pushed her away and started crying,' Mrs Krebs said. 'I begged my husband to leave me alone. I was kicking and shouting and I didn't want to be touched.'

'He pulled down the duvet and tried to open my thighs. He was trying to have intercourse with me and at that stage I told him to go to Pat if that was what he wanted,'... which is exactly what her husband did.

At this point, Mrs Krebs became so angry, she hit him on the shoulder with a vase. When he still refused to stop, she picked up the bottle of wine he had brought into the room and smashed it over his head. There was a brief fight, after which Mrs Krebs ran into the bathroom and locked herself in the shower. Her husband went after her. He got hold of a hammer and used it to destroy the shower door.

Miss du Preez claimed that the shower door was intact when she left the house. She agreed that the Krebs had had a violent argument and that Mrs Krebs smashed a bottle of wine over her husband's head.

'He was shouting and swearing at me. He told me to come out. He said he would kill me. He was furious, angry,' said Mrs Krebs.

After failing to get the shower door open, Mr Krebs went away. Mrs Krebs went back into the bedroom, but there was no one there. She saw her husband's gun lying in a cupboard and picked it up.

'I wanted to make it safe,' she explained. 'I wanted to look at it to see if it was loaded.'

She was still holding the gun when Miss du Preez came into the room.

'I didn't threaten to harm or kill Pat,' she said. 'I never saw her again after that,' she added.

Seconds later, her husband came into the room. Mrs Krebs said that she was so scared of him she ran out of the main bedroom door and down the passage.

'I ran down the steps and turned around because the front door was closed. He was at the top of the steps. I told him not to come any closer and to leave me alone.

'I was holding the gun with both hands against my chest to steady it. Suddenly, there was a loud noise. My husband touched his chest and sighed.'

After shooting her husband she ran out into the night.

'I was very frightened. I ran to the next door neighbours...'

By 10 March, both the prosecution and the defence concluded their arguments. Over the weekend that followed, Mr Justice Vermooten retired to consider his verdict.

On the morning of Monday, 13 March, he acquitted Maria Krebs of the charge of murdering her husband and found her guilty of culpable homicide. She was fined R2 000 (or one year's imprisonment), and sentenced to a further three years imprisonment, suspended for five years. She was declared unfit to carry a firearm, but aquitted on the charge of attempted murder.

Only in France is a crime passionnel, or crime of passion, a legally-recognised defence. In South Africa, a murder committed in a moment of passion is seen as a mitigating circumstance and does not merit special treatment. If the court accepts the view that the crime was committed during a moment of passion, then this usually means that an accusation of murder is reduced to a lesser charge, such as culpable homicide.

There were gasps of surprise and some spontaneous clapping when Mr Justice Vermooten handed down the sentence.

In his summing-up, Mr Justice Vermooten said the court believed Maria Krebs' version of the events of the night of 21 October, 1987, rather than that of Miss du Preez.

In his judgment, Mr Justice Vermooten said that Miss du Preez' evidence was rejected except where it was corroborated by other witnesses. He said that Miss du Preez was only one witness and that her evidence was full of contradictions. Her testimony fell short of the requirements for the acceptance of a single witness.

Mr Justice Vermooten also added, 'It is an untruth that the money was not the important thing. She said she was prepared to go out to anyone for no money, which is a blatant untruth as this was her livelihood.'

Furthermore, he added, there were two facts which corroborated Mrs Krebs' version of the incident.

'Firstly, the broken state of the shower cubicle door showed a vicious attack on her by Mr Krebs, and secondly, she arrived at the neighbour's place naked, which showed a state of extreme shock.'

After sentencing, the court was also told that Mrs Krebs had a previous conviction for possession of pornography. This was mentioned only after sentencing, as it was thought to be prejudicial evidence. In January 1986, she had been fined R300 or 30 days. Mrs Krebs maintained that the offence was committed by her husband, but that she had taken the rap on his behalf since he was a German national and stood the possibility of being deported.

And so the three-in-a-bed trial ended – but the story wasn't quite finished. While Maria Krebs did all in her power to retire from the public eye, Miss du Preez first sold her story to *Scope* magazine and was then interviewed on M-Net's *Carte Blanche* by Ruda Landman.

'I am full of regret,' she admitted. 'The trial has changed my life and I have left prostitution behind me.'